Amy Carmichael

MIMOSA

A True Story

Amy
Carmichael

MIMOSA

A True Story

PUBLICATIONS
Fort Washington, PA 19034

Mimosa
Published by CLC Publications

U.S.A.
P.O. Box 1449, Fort Washington, PA 19034

UNITED KINGDOM
CLC International (UK)
Unit 5, Glendale Avenue, Sandycroft, Flintshire, CH5 2QP

ISBN-13 (trade paper): 978-0-87508-821-1
ISBN-13 (e-book): 978-1-936143-57-3

First published 1924
by S.P.C.K.
London

This printing 2015
by permission of
Dohnavur Fellowship

Italics in Scripture quotations are the emphasis of the author

Contents

Foreword

THIS story is true. It tells the eternally new tale of the matchless charm of our Lord Jesus Christ. One look at that loveliness, and, though the one who looked did not even remember His name, she was His forever.

The story came to us at a time of disappointment and temptation to downheartedness. And mightily it cheered us. It spoke in a clear, glad voice, and it said, "Fear not at all. Where your hands cannot reach and your love cannot help, His hands can reach and His love can help. So why are you afraid?"

And it said that miles of space and solid walls and locked doors are nothing to Love. Nothing at all.

And it said—and we set it down with a great hope that it may cheer some other, for it said it very earnestly—"The seed is not your poor little word. *The seed is the Word of God.*"

Amy Carmichael
Dohnavur, 1924

Chapter One

Mimosa

$\mathcal{S}$HE was standing out in the sunshine when I first saw her, a radiant thing in a crimson and orange sari, and many bright bangles. She looked like a bird from the woods in her colors and her jewels, but her eyes were large and soft and gentle, more like a fawn's than a bird's.

We welcomed her and her tall father, who stood beside her; but there was always an inward misgiving in our welcome to that father, for his little daughter, Star, was with us, and though he had consented to her staying with us, he might at any time retrieve her.

---

*With what eagerness
we searched the two men's faces as we entered.*

How present the past may be: it is as if he stood before me now, that upright, valiant Hindu, with his clear-cut face and piercing eyes, every line of him expressing a fixed determination. I see the Iyer (Walker of Tinnevelly) meeting him with a friendly gesture of welcome (to shake hands would have been pollution). I see the two men, so apart yet so alike in certain traits of character, walking through the living room to the side room used as a study.

Then after a little there came a call, and the two girls and I went together to the other room. With what eagerness we searched the two men's faces as we entered. And then flamed past a burning half-hour, and at last—time after time this happened—the father would rise, and towering above his older daughter stretch out his hand to take her, and down would fall his arm.

"What is it? What power is it?
It is as if a paralysis were upon me."

"What is it? What power is it? It is as if a paralysis were upon me," he said once.

And we told him: "The Lord God of heaven and earth has marked this child for His. It is His will that she should learn of Him." And he bowed to the word and allowed her to stay a little longer.

But nothing could prevail upon him to leave the younger one, Mimosa. We were keeping caste as regarded Star—every scrupulous observance was being kept, for we had not the right to allow her to break the law of her family. We would have done the same for Mimosa. But no, she might not stay.

The child, who in that one afternoon had heard what drew her very soul in passionate longing to hear more, pleaded earnestly:

"Oh, father, just for a little while that I may understand a little, only a very little, and I will return."

"Wouldst thou shame me, O foolish one? Is not one shame enough?"

Again she pleaded, all her shyness of her stern father and all fear of offence melted in the strong fires of desire.

"Oh, father, father!"

But he turned on her, indignant: "Look at thy sister. Is not one shame enough, I say?" and he withered her with his wrath.

There was silence for a moment. Then Mimosa burst into tears.

The farewells were soon said. As they were going away the child turned, and I saw the little figure in its bird-breast raiment against the dark green shadows of the mango trees. Dashing the tears from her eyes, she tried to smile to us; and my last memory of her—and it has lived all these twenty-two years—is of big, beautiful brown eyes trying to smile through tears.

And we? We went back to the duty of the day and tried not to be downcast; but the child had been more than usually intelligent; and she had listened with such a sweet and charmed attention to the little we had time to tell her that we could all but hear the Lover of children say: "Suffer her to come unto Me." Would they allow her to come? If only we might have taught her more of Him! How could she possibly remember what we had told her? It was impossible to expect her to remember.

Impossible? Is there such a word where the things of the Lord are concerned?

Chapter Two

Let the Stick Dance

"SOMETHING has happened to the child. What is the matter with her?"

The speaker, Mimosa's mother, was angry. And when that mother was angry the stick danced.

"Look at her, not a vestige of the holy ashes has she smeared on her forehead."

"What will the neighbors say?" It was an aunt who was speaking now.

"Come, thou little ingrate, come here this moment!" The child came, but she stood silent.

"The child is bewitched. Look at her!
She has drunk of the magic medicine of the white people."

Then the mother, the aunt, the older sisters, and anyone who happened to be passing, talked to her. They talked all at once, and they all talked loudly. The house was full of their clamor. They talked promiscuously to each other and to her, and hurled proverbs like little pellets at her head.

"The child is bewitched. Look at her! She has drunk of the magic medicine of the white people."

"Yea, she is charmed. There is a charm in the white people's talk. Charmed? She is spoiled. 'The spoiled child fears not the word,' as the saying is. Let her taste the rod."

"Like the help of the rod what help is there?" Then all together: "Will the child that fears not the reproving eye fear the chastening hand? Nevertheless feel it she must."

"The twig unbent within five years, will it be bent at fifty?"

"The unbeaten bull, will it be broken to its work?"

"The undisciplined and the untwirled moustache, will they attain prosperity?"

At last, exasperated by the child's silence—for Mimosa did not know what to say, having already said all she knew—the mother carried her off and administered the correction so urgently required. And the little girl cried softly to herself and wondered at the strangeness of everything. She had tried to tell them, and they could not understand.

What had she tried to tell them?

It is difficult to say, just because there was not much to tell. But something had happened on that afternoon when she heard for the first time about a living, loving God, whom we had called Father, who had made everything in the world, and the sun and moon and stars. She had understood that He loved her. And a strange thing had happened. Though there was no time to tell her much of the Lord Jesus Christ, some sense as of seeing a Great Love, feeling it indeed, as one does feel love without being able to explain it, had come upon her, so that she loved this loving One, knew He loved her—though of what had been done to reveal that love to man she knew just nothing;

there had not been time to tell her. Only she knew some-how that just as the blue air was round about her that afternoon as she walked back with her father, so that when she looked up she could see blue beyond blue, so the love of this wonderful God was about her and above her, and everywhere was love. Tell it in terms of ordinary speech and you find yourself floating off into shoreless, sound-less, timeless seas—what that child had seen that day was as much as a child could see of the Eternal Love. Charmed? Yes, they told the truth who said it. This book is the tale of a soul that was charmed.

The question of rubbing Siva's ashes on her forehead, or refusing to rub them, had, of course, not been touched upon at all that afternoon. But when she went home, and as usual the basket containing them was handed to her in the morning as the family custom was, she shrank back, feeling instinctively that she could not rub those ashes on now. They meant allegiance to Siva. Siva was not her God now. She had another God, even the Loving One.

It was this unaccountable refusal which had first per-plexed, then enraged her family. The basket, with the ashes which the father brought once a month from the temple, was hung from a beam in the living room. Every morning the father and his sons smeared the ashes on brow, arms, and breast. And the mother and daughters smeared them on their foreheads. To go out of doors without that mark on was disgrace.

The family bore it for a day or two, then, in the more tolerant father's absence, the women determined to end it. Mimosa had struggled through a lame little explanation, but she could not show them what she had seen, and her faltering words had failed. She had stood among them

> "Dumb to their scorn, and turning on their
> laughter
> Only the dominance of earnest eyes."

But that dominance was too spiritual to appeal just then. The day came when it did. At that moment it was sheer naughtiness or bewitchment, or both mixed. Anyhow, there was only one thing to do. "As the stick dances, the monkey must dance. Let the stick dance." And it danced.

Chapter Three

I Could Be Crucified Once

*S*O passed several uncomfortable years. Mimosa acquired a tiresome trick of shrugging her shoulders, and "answering back"; for she did not by any means grow into a sweet little saint all at once, and the rather frequent and sometimes severe chastisements left her sometimes in a very unsaintlike frame of mind. It was all so bewildering. If God—the God to whom she clung the more fiercely because of these sharp smitings, little limpet that she was—were indeed as she had heard and believed, living and powerful and loving, why did He not keep her mother's hands off the whisk which was her favorite instrument of correction? It was a question that found no answer. Was the child forgotten by the Love that had shone upon her?

She knew . . . that the God
she would not forsake had not forsaken her.

Love never forgets. Gradually through her troubles a gentle sense of still being loved stole in upon her soul. She knew, though how she could never have told, that the God she would not forsake had not forsaken her. And all alone, without a single friend who understood, or a single touch of human compassion, she was comforted. And gradually she learned patience, learned to accept her discipline.

"Then came the time when I went into *maraivu.*" This was not tyranny, it was only the custom of the caste. The word means seclusion, and the custom springs from fear. For when the Mohammedan conquests changed the ways of the old Hindus, they felt the secluded life safer for their growing-up girls, and to this day, just when the mind in her is all one eager question, the child is shut up within narrow limits. And there that child stays till her marriage releases her.

"Didst thou ever break through and run out?"

"No, never; how could I? The Rule is to stay in."

"But how didst thou endure it?"

"There was no other way but to endure it."

"Does no girl ever break the Rule?"

"Never, never." And Mimosa added, what translated into modern English would be: "It's not done."

And she was such a vivid girl. Into her at her creation her Maker had inspired a soul that inclines to activity, and breathed a vital spirit. But this activity of vitality displeased her elders, who disapproved of "learned girls." Learning was for boys. So Mimosa was cooped up in small rooms and set to small tasks, and heard only the smallest of small talk, and the inquiring mind crowded with questions was treated as a freak. "What is that to thee? Art thou not a woman-child?" Thus passed the dull, drab years.

She had much to endure. Sometimes it was as if the winds that blew about her had blown out the one little candle that stood unsheltered in the midst of them. Several times she yielded and bowed before the idols. These were her darkest periods. But she was not forsaken; the Love that followed found her. And then, all the more because she had weakened, the full blast of trial fell on her again.

"I could be crucified once," said Neesama-san of Japan, and he was a man at liberty, strong, and with full knowledge. "But this daily crucifixion!" And now something hardly less was appointed for this Indian girl who had heard so little, and was to hear nothing for many years. Is not the courage of the love of God amazing? Could human love have asked it of a soul? Fortitude based on knowledge so slender; deathless, dauntless faith—who could have dared to ask it but the Lord God Himself? And what could have held her but Love Omnipotent? We have yet to prove more bravely the forces of that love.

Chapter Four

I Go to the Supreme

"NAY, to this assembly I go not."

It was the father, head of the family and clan, who spoke, and he spoke with decision; but never a thought that he was bidden to another assembly came to the daughters and relatives as they donned their best and brightest attire and set forth with crowds of caste folk from their own village and numbers of others to attend the great festival at the temple by the sea, one of the chief pilgrimages of the year.

All his life he had thought of Siva as Lord of the soul; and he had thought of his soul as an animal fettered in his flesh. His soul belonged to Siva as an animal belongs to its master—but the fetter of the flesh had bound it. All he had done in the course of his religious life had, stated simply, but one object. His prime business was to loosen the fetters of this bound soul that it might be restored to its owner.

And to secure an education for his two sons he had let them eat of Christian food.

And now that which would forever free it from this fetter of the flesh was upon him, and he looked death in the face.

He had worshiped in scores of temples, given alms, daily rubbed the sacred ashes, the *Vibuthi*, on brow, breast, arms; had traced, in so far as mortal might, the intricate labyrinth of the 1,008 names and attributes of his god; and had worshiped Siva's wife and sons, whose images were everywhere to be seen in wayside shrine and Saivite temple. To make all safe, he had sacrificed to countless demons; there was nothing he could think of that he had left undone, nor had he ever done those things which he ought not to have done except in the matter of his daughter Star: he had yielded to her vain desire. And to secure an education for his two sons he had let them eat of Christian food.

And now all that was left was to gather into one last symbolic act his whole life's faith. And Mimosa, trembling, saw her mother bring the box of sacred ashes to him. "Mark the *Vibuthi*," she said. With it thick and white upon him, the dread God of death would know him for Siva's own.

But he put the ashes from him. There were no explanations. He was too ill for that. He only waved the box aside and, looking into the face of death, cried, "I go to the Supreme," and so passed.

Then was done according to custom.

The departed spirit is not regarded by the Hindus as having passed beyond the reach of our care, and so at once, especially in the case of a parent, everything that love can suggest is done to help it. This thought is behind all and gives a dignity to the ceremonies that follow swift-footed upon death.

Quickly, in a little shelter improvised in the courtyard, Mimosa's father was laid on a mat, and shaved, and bathed with water hurriedly brought from the nearest river—the sacred copper-colored river which the Greeks named long ago.

A white muslin cloth was wrapped round him now, and the consecrated ashes he had refused were rubbed on brow, breast, and arms. Then a ball of rice was laid on his mouth, and on it friends put silver coins. This was to help his disembodied spirit on the first part of its journey.

And then the weeping, wailing women, led by Mimosa's mother, walked round and round the body, throwing their arms up, beating their breasts, tearing their loosened hair, which fell in black masses about them. And they sat down on the ground, and, rocking backwards and forwards, chanted the song that compares the dead man to all that is strong and glorious and dear. No one can sit through such a scene unmoved. It is the stuff that grief is made of, the grief that has no hope.

All this our little Mimosa heard and shared. But she was too dazed to chant, too stunned for tears. And when they carried her father forth to perform the remaining ceremonies at the cremation ground, while the conch shell was blown and a band of many instruments blared in deafening chorus, she felt that the walls of her whole life were falling down about her.

Chapter Five

Parpom

$\mathscr{T}$HE next event of supreme importance to Mimosa was her wedding.

On the day when she was telling me about it we were together in my room, along whose wall stand several bookcases.

"I will show the colors of my saris," said Mimosa, rising and going to one of the bookcases. "I had one like *this*"—she pointed to Trevelyan's *Garibaldi* (bright red)— "and one like this"—*Tennyson and His Friends* (bright green) —"and this"—it was *The China Martyrs of 1900,* in orange-yellow. A prolonged search from bookcase to bookcase followed, and finally she discovered *Kim* (crimson) and *Lord Kelvin's Life* (terracotta-brown), which fairly satisfied her.

But soon to the startled girl the word
began to be whispered: All was not as it appeared.

And she had had plenty of jewels. Her brass was the best of its kind. For all these necessary things her father had left provision. The long, warm day saw her early at the well, with her dark hair parted smoothly and her pretty garments and bright jewels making her more than ever a bird of radiant plumage. And as the sun rose on her as she stood there, a seventeen-year-old bride, he must have loved to light her like a picture, with the old grey well for foreground and the wide sky for frame.

But soon to the startled girl the word began to be whispered: All was not as it appeared. She was poor.

It was true. Her husband, advised by his elder brother, a clever, unprincipled scoundrel, had deceived Mimosa's mother. He was not only landless, he was neck-deep in debt.

In Mimosa's family the custom was for the bridegroom to endow the bride with a substantial gift of land before marriage. This the bridegroom had done. It was the only land he had, but, of course, Mimosa's mother had no idea of this.

Mimosa went to him. He worshiped the ground she walked on (her own idiom; so East and West touch sometimes). When he was with her she could do as she would with him. The trouble was that he was generally with his elder brother, who then held the reins. Mimosa, however, had character and would not be silenced. "I cannot sleep while we owe one farthing," she said.

But this was absurd. Why should she not be able to sleep? What folly possessed her? It was altogether shocking, and he did so dislike shocks.

Now the neighbors, though they had been quiet for a while after the wedding, had not forgotten that Mimosa was not a worshiper of the usual gods. And they were sure mischief would come of it; the marriage would be unlucky. "*Parpom*," * they had said. "We shall see." And they had

---

* Pronounced "*pair-pome*."

twisted their hands, palms uppermost (in a curious way impossible to show in words) and waved them to and fro as if trying to wave off the impending ill-luck. "*Parpom;* yes, *Parpom.*"

Then the helpful elder brother came to the rescue. If Mimosa felt so, there was only one thing to be done. Let her sell her marriage portion, the land now written to her name. Mimosa eagerly consented, and it was done. The brother kindly helped in the transaction, and did not lose by it.

But, landless, how were they to live?

Mimosa went again to her husband, and spoke words that sounded like thunderclaps in his pained, astonished ears.

"Let us work," she said.

And he gazed at her, half grieved and half admiring, for she was a very lovely vision with her vivid face and her golden jewels, and her little delicate hands and feet. On her arms and ankles were silver bangles hung with little bells that tinkled when she moved. Yes, she was very desirable, that could not be denied.

But flower of delight as his bride might be, she was most perniciously peculiar. What was to be done? Never in his dreamiest dreams had he conceived so strange a thing. Work! Did she say, "Let us work"? But he had never worked, had never thought of working.

What was debt? Would not the sons that were to be pay it off? The interest—yes, that was a worrisome item, but, even so, it could accumulate. Let it be. This, up till now, had been his attitude. Now he found himself more or less unwillingly denuded of that rather admirable glory of debt. (If you have no debt, does it not follow that no one trusts you enough to lend you anything, and from that is it not obvious that you are a person of small consequence?) This new proposal staggered him; it would have been so much easier to slide into debt again. But he agreed. Yes, they would work.

The brother-in-law suggested merchandise. That was pleasant. You had only to sit in your little shop-front, one of a dozen such in the bazaar, and wait till people came in to buy. Salt was to be his commodity—easy to store, easy to ladle out. So he agreed.

But money was needed to start even a salt bazaar, and the ever-helpful brother had a brilliant idea. There were Mimosa's dowry jewels, gathered one by one through careful years by her father. There was especially her great golden garland, the most costly of all. Sell these and start in salt! To earn an honest livelihood Mimosa gave them all.

They were all lost, every jewel of that heap was lost. The brother had wise ways of losing such treasure. Mimosa could do nothing to recover them.

There was hardly anything left that she could sell. The little she could lay her hands on she gathered and gave to her mother; neither husband nor brother-in-law could be trusted to keep it for her. And her mother promised to dole out a small sum every month. When the time came to give it, the mother refused.

"Thou gave thy dowry jewels to thy husband! Even the golden garland! No worthy daughter of mine art thou. No money shalt thou have of me. Let thy God help thee!"

The village heard it and smiled. "Did we not say *Parpom*?"

Chapter Six

I Am Not Offended With You

*T*HEN Mimosa went out into the fields. In her arms lay her first-born son, for the blow had fallen upon her in a weak hour. She had never heard of Hagar; but in her grief she walked in Hagar's steps. She hung her baby in a strip of cotton stuff and tied it to the branch of an acacia tree. For a minute or two she swung the hammock gently till he slept, and then she went away alone and sat down over against him a good way off, and she cried unto the Lord.

Not one scripture did she know;
there was nothing from the Book of books
for the Spirit to take and show her at that moment.
— But His resources are limitless! —

She had never learned to pray, never heard prayer except when we committed her to the love of the Lord, before we said good-bye. In Tamil we have four forms of the pronoun in the second person. There is *thou,* used by older to younger and superior to inferior; there is a second singular form, a trifle more deferential. The third is used generally from, say, child to father, and properly translated *you*; and there is one higher still, translated by such words as "your honor," "your excellency." In Tamil classic poetry, with a wonderful instinct for eternal values, the lowest of all, *thou,* is used in addressing the Deity, who is recognized to transcend earth's poor titles of respect. The Christian usage is to employ the slightly higher singular form.

Mimosa knew nothing of the classics, nor did she know Christian usage, so to her the most natural word was that which she would have used in speaking to her father; she said *you.*

"O God," she said aloud, and the words seemed to rise through the thin blue air above her, "O God, my husband has deceived me, his brother has deceived me, even my mother has deceived me, but You will not deceive me."

Then she waited a little, looking up, and stretching out her arms, declared: "Yes, they have all deceived me, but I am not offended with You. Whatever You do is good. What should I do without You? You are the Giver of health and strength and will to work. Are not these things better than riches or people's help?" And again she waited a while.

Then, kneeling there in the open field, she drew the loose end of her sari around and spread it out, holding it open before the Lord. In some such way Ruth must have held her mantle when Boaz poured into it six measures of barley. To the Eastern women it means all that ever can be expressed of humble loving expectation: "For he said, 'Go not empty.'" Thus Mimosa knelt: "*You* will not deceive me."

The sun beat down on her; the little young cotton plants about her drooped their soft green leaves, but she knelt on, heeding nothing, her sari still spread out before her God: "I am an emptiness for You to fill."

Not one scripture did she know; there was nothing

from the Book of books for the Spirit to take and show to her at that moment. But His resources are limitless, and back to her troubled mind came the memory of a wise word of her father's: *"He who planted the tree will water it."* Yes, God was her heavenly Gardener. Had He not planted His little tree? Would He not water it? She dropped her sari and rose.

Then what happened? Was it, as in that older story, that God opened her eyes, and she saw a well of water and went and drank of it? Suddenly all her weariness passed. She knew herself refreshed, invigorated. He had heard; her God had heard. She was not battling along as best she could, lonely, desolate. She had her God. "Oh, what should I do without You?" The words rose like a triumph song. With the little gesture of the folded hands which is the universal Indian *Amen,* she bowed her head, and stood a moment drinking from the waters of comfort. And then she went to the tree where her baby swung in the light wind, and, taking him from it, threw the wisp of cloth across her shoulders and walked back to her home filled with a peace that passed her understanding.

Chapter Seven

The Tulasi Plant

*A*ND now a gallant purpose formed in her. To the west of the village lay the cotton fields that had belonged to her family. Some still belonged to her relatives. She would work there like any coolie woman, and earn money to sustain her husband and boy. And this she did, in sun and wind; and, what was far harder, she worked in the stuffy little courtyards where the piles of cotton were flung in heaps to be carded, breathing the fluff-laden, stifling air for days on end. Ten minutes in one of those courtyards sends one out half choked. Mimosa spent an age of minutes there.

The years were piled with pain.
Every indignity which ingenuity could devise
was heaped upon her.

What inspired her, who can tell? She had never heard the command to owe no man anything. The traditions of her country lay towards debt, not from it. Her husband, the responsible one, saw nothing uncomfortable in sitting down in it. Perhaps it was the delicate purity of her mind, perhaps the effect of the light from the lighted candle the winds had not blown out; whatever it was, it carried her through years of hard living, and never once through all those years did her hands drop to her sides in despair.

But the years were piled with pain. Every indignity which ingenuity could devise was heaped upon her. For India, kind land as she is in many of her aspects, can be very cruel to one who crosses her law of caste and custom, and a worshiper of a strange God is not beloved in a conservative community.

The tulasi plant is sacred through all India. It is a small, inconspicuous basil and it grows wild everywhere. Some hold that it is pervaded with the essence of Vishnu and his wife Lakshmi, and it is considered to be a deity in itself. Others say it is Sita, Rama's wife, one of the beautiful Indian women of story. Others say it embodies all the deities in its fragile, fragrant stems and leaves and tiny, unpretentious flowers and fruit. Monier Williams believes it certain that it is the object of more adoration than any other plant in India, and so in all the world. And he quotes the prayer to it: "I adore that tulasi in whose roots are all the sacred places of pilgrimage, in whose center are all the deities, and in whose upper branches are the Vedas." Every day millions of Indian women, to whom it specially seems to belong, walk around it, in its little pot set in the midst of their courtyard or in the temple. And they offer rice and flowers to it, and the childless wife drinks a concoction made of its leaves chopped fine and mixed with water, and the snake-bitten finds healing in its juice.

In Mimosa's village it is more feared than worshiped; for all the people there are Saivites and, though worshipers of Siva consider it sacred, it is not to them what it is to worshipers of Vishnu or Rama (one of Vishnu's incarnations), and so it comes to pass that the plant in that part of the country is left to grow and multiply as it likes in the fields; no one touches it for fear of enraging the gods, and it is not enough used in worship to put any check on its growth.

Mimosa saw it growing in masses of aromatic clusters. She badly needed firewood. Its slender stems do not suggest fuel, but dried they would serve her need. If the one true God had made it—her living God—was it His desire that it should waste itself in the fields? But to use it for kindling? Who would dare?

She dared. One day she carried home a huge armful of it, and spread it to dry in her courtyard. The horrified women gathered round.

"The vengeance of the gods!"

"Oh, bitterly they will avenge themselves on thee!"

"Stay, stay, thou fool woman! Touch it not. Burn the tulasi of the angry gods? Disaster will follow; the curse will fall!"

The clamor grew about her. She stood quiet in the midst: "But these gods are not as my God. There is one great God, one only. How, then, can the lesser gods avenge themselves upon me? He whom I worship is Creator of the tulasi."

It was a wonderful chance to witness to the truth she held. But the women were furious and terrified too—not hurt in heart, else she could not have touched the plant. It was not affection that sharpened their abuse, it was fear; fear of the vengeance of the offended powers.

Mimosa used her fuel and, to the surprise of the village, nothing immediately happened. But they still said, "*Parpom.*"

And she was a derision daily.

Chapter Eight

Mayil, Little Peacock

*H*ER second baby was such a lovely little fellow that she called him Mayil, "little peacock"; for the thought of that gorgeous bird to this color-loving people is not spoiled by foolish human talk of pride being somewhere in the heart of it. "Little peacock" meant just beauty, and the joy of it. Her "golden boy," she called him, too; and the word was hardly too adoring, for the smooth velvet of such a baby's skin is not just brown—indeed, hardly brown at all. It is full of warm light, like sunlight seen through water on brown stones; and the eyes with their long curled lashes, and the little red mouth, are so many distinct delights.

---

*And then with a heavy heart
she would go out to the fields; . . .
and those two babies were left alone,
a two-and-a-half to tend a six-months.*

What of the scorn of the village now? It was nothing, just nothing. For six blessed months she nursed her little treasure, taking him out with her to the fields, hanging his hammock to a branch of a tree, going to him now and then as her work allowed; and he throve in the pure air and grew in loveliness every day.

Then the rainy season came, and she could not take him out with her. Kinglet, her first-born, was now two-and-a-half, and, after doing the work of the house, she used to hang Mayil in his hammock, tie a rope to it, set a pillow on the floor, put a bowl of food beside it, and say to Kinglet: "Stay, little one, and sit there. Here is rice; eat it when hunger comes to thee. If thy little brother cries, see, here is a rope, pull his cradle back and forth till he be quiet. Be good till I return."

And then with a heavy heart (but what else could she do?) she would go out to the fields; and from nine in the morning till six in the evening those two babies were left alone, a two-and-a-half to tend a six-months.

Wet to the skin and weary, she would return at sunset and go straight to her poor baby. But those eight hours without food or drink left him greatly exhausted, and her tears would fall on his face as she nestled him in her arms and tried to make up to him for all he had been missing. Till the wet season was over, this was the daily routine. Not a neighbor, not a relative, offered to see to her poor little boys while she was out.

But this did not seem strange to her. "What would you expect? I was not a woman of the Way, nor was I a Hindu woman." And that seemed reason enough to give. Why should anyone have helped her? She was not as they. And the patience in her face was like the glow one sees on the mountains when the clouds that hang about them in the evening deepen the quiet beauty of valley and ravine.

But her poor little Mayil never quite recovered from his unmothered days. He was as frail as a flower of the heat that grows up somehow through the red clod, but is never like the sturdy flower of the rain. He was tall and slim, and his beautiful eyes were like stars. He would never leave his mother, once he had her, without bitter crying and clinging, and she dreaded having to part with him for an hour. When he was older, and could sit by her while she did her cooking, he would play contentedly if only he might have the end of her sari in his hand.

But he was as happy as a bird, and like a bird he sang his own little songs that he made for himself.

"What rice today, mother?" he would ask. And she would tell him. And then he would begin to croon a line or two, to a tune of his own.

"What singest thou, little peacock?" she would ask him.

"I sing a song of the rice," he would answer.

And then he would take three pebbles like her three cooking stones and lay a shard of pottery upon them. "See, I too am cooking rice. I blow the fire, I fill the pot, I cook the rice. See, I cook it, and I sing to it!" And he would play and sing, happy to be near her. "He could not bear to be without me," said his mother.

He did not learn to walk soon. Someone suggested planting his little feet in the earth, like two little trees. "Plant them deep. Make the holes deep, up to his knees, and press the earth down. Then will he be compelled to stand, and finally will walk."

But Mimosa thought it a cruel way, and instead contrived a small pushcart out of some odd pieces of wood, and he learned to walk at last.

Chapter Nine

Boaz

*B*UT before he could walk, another little one came who was to grow up to be her very heart's joy. Music, as we see him now, is a child so sensitive, so pure of spirit, that the verse about the children's angels comes constantly to mind. But his life, like his little brother's, had its early troubles. His mother was very ill, and lay in weakness and in loneliness so profound that Kinglet, then barely five years old, and her husband—who, though so futile, was not an unkind man, and who just then was at home with her—were her only nurses, her only help.

When her baby was ten days old she called her husband. He had not noticed how day by day the little store of grain grew less. He walked in a sleepy dream. But for Mimosa no such dreams might be; she knew to an ounce how much rice there was. She had counted on being able to work by now. But the will that had carried her through so much was helpless before this onslaught of great weakness.

"I cannot go to the fields," she said, "but will you not go to the town by the sea"—and she named it—"and tell my youngest brother how things are? Tell him I am weak, but will return anything he may send. Ask him for the loan of two rupees; two only will suffice." And she sent him off.

This younger brother had been well educated, even as the elder brother (of whom we shall hear later) had been. And once, during the long holidays when he was ill here, we had nursed him day and night. He, like his elder brother, had been baptized; but, like him, though continuing a Christian in name, he had long ago turned back to the husks.

Mimosa knew this. "He has never spoken to me of that which he once believed, but surely he cannot have forgotten all? Surely he will be kind," she thought. He had obtained well-paying work as a result of the education given by Christians' money. Would he begrudge two rupees of it to help her? She would return it; he knew she would return it.

But after her husband had gone she lay and thought about it. She had never before asked anyone for anything. She felt doubtful. Had she made a mistake?

There was a side room at one end of the house. It had no windows, only a door opening off the inner verandah. She kept her stores of grain there, when there were stores to keep. She used the room for prayer, for it was quiet, remote from the noise of the street.

When I heard this story, the passing of the years had softened its outlines; but when I asked Mimosa what else was in the room, her eyes filled with the sweetest smile.

"Why, nothing," she said, "nothing but quite empty earthen vessels. Nothing else at all was in that room that day."

She rose slowly from her mat and, leaning on the wall for support, went to the room, taking her baby with her and calling to the other two little boys to come. They left their play and followed her in. Then she partly shut the door—not quite, lest the darkness should trouble the children—and with her arms around them she told her Father just what she had done, how she had never done so before, how she would understand if it could not be as she had asked, how she would know then that He had some other way to come to her relief. "And it will be well, Father; however You do it, it will be well."

Her husband returned. The walk to and fro of thirty miles had been for nothing, for he had not brought back any money. "No," the younger brother had said, forgetting the kind ways of his land, "she is weak. How can I know she will ever be strong enough to work and return it?"

"O Father, it cannot be
that Your little ones are to be hungry,
and yet it appears to be so.
I do not understand it, BUT it is well."

Then Mimosa took her three little ones into that dim room again. The larger empty pots stood on the floor, the smaller ones were heaped in a corner. "Father, it is well," she said. "All that You do is well."

But the children's food? She paused for a minute, then in their hearing said: "O Father, it cannot be that Your little ones are to be hungry, and yet it appears to be so. I do not understand it, but it is well." And she led them out of the empty room and shut the door.

Now, among her relatives was one, only a distant relative, but so connected that for her to work in his fields was as if Ruth worked in the barleyfields of Boaz; and he was a kind and a just man. He had observed Mimosa; he knew that, wherever she was, the work was done faithfully, and there was no need to oversee it. He came now to inquire when he might hope to have her back again.

She told him that she could not say when she could return, for she could not regain her strength.

"Then send thy husband" was his not unnatural rejoinder; and he would have departed, but, noticing her thin, tired face, he drew the truth from her.

"This cannot be! I will not let it be!" he exclaimed. And he sent at once a supply for six days, enough to stir up the poor, slack husband to turn his hand to some honest work, so that the loan was soon returned. This was enough to cheer the soul of the wife, who saw in it the loving hand of her God. Once more she and her children went into the dark little room, now furnished with grain, and to her grateful faith it was an illuminated place.

Chapter Ten

Did She Not Burn the Tulasi?

*L*ITTLE MAYIL was three, and his small brother, a chubby, glowing baby, had just begun to find his way all over the house on eager, uncertain little feet when one evening at dusk, while she prepared the evening meal, Mimosa was startled by a cry from her husband and ran to him on the outer verandah. "See, see! A thorn has run into my right foot's ankle!"

But there was no thorn; it must have been a snake. No snake could be found. It had stung the foot and then glided off into the twilight.

"A snake! A snake!"

"A snake! A snake!" No call in all India can more quickly gather a crowd. In the twinkling of an eye, it seemed, the house was full of people, commiserating, inquiring, advising, declaiming, prophesying death and destruction. It was only the usual crowd that attends upon all excitements and completes all confusions; but in and out of it and through it ran real emotion, real distress. Relatives wailed aloud, women tore their hair and beat themselves, and violently knocked their heads against whatever hard thing lay near. To everyone, poor Mimosa's husband was as good as dead.

Meanwhile, thus encouraged, the poison "ascended to the skull" until the bitten man was in desperate pain, "as if the bones were being cleft in two," and the sympathetic clamor waxed louder and more excited, and the street filled as half the village turned out to mourn and lament his rapidly approaching death.

And in the midst was Mimosa, doing what she could to relieve him, paying no heed to the sibilant whisper that presently began to fill the room like the hissing of a snake. "It is she! It is she! It is she that has swallowed her husband's life. It is she! It is she! *Did she not burn the tulasi?*"

The excitement subsided, for her husband did not die, but lay very ill and tormented with pain, and she knelt by the stricken man and prayed, crying to her God, the God of gods. Then she went into the little dark room and held out her sari in supplication to Him. And she nursed him with all the skill she knew, putting on poultices of fine-chopped rice straw, and feeding him with tempting food. And her faithful, tender heart rejoiced exceedingly when at last he was out of danger of death; but he was blind and he was mad. Crazy and blind on her brave hands!

Chapter Eleven

Seed Corn

*I*T was just then, then in her desperate hour, that succor came.

There were a few Christian families in the village, but none of them took any notice of Mimosa; for, with the exception of one family, they were of another caste, and they were all of the kind known as "Name-Christians." It is easy to blame them and wonder at their lovelessness; but if they had interfered in her affairs it is not likely they could have continued to live peacefully in the village. Her caste would have made life most unpleasant for them. Only a very ardent love will face things being made uncomfortable, and is ardent love found everywhere? The one Christian family belonging to Mimosa's caste was confessedly nominal—Christian only because the grandfather and grandmother had joined the Way years ago, and, being conservative in feeling, the family stayed on in the religion. But between its kind of Christianity and Hinduism pure and simple there had never been much of a hedge, and the hedge, such as it was, had many gaps now, through which one might comfortably creep. To such, a converted, enlightened Mimosa would have been very unwelcome.

But the old granny who was *not* "nominal" still lived. Her picture, drawn once for all, will be found in Faber's "Old Laborer."

"What doth God get from him?
    His very mind is dim,
Too weak to love, and too obtuse to fear.
    Is there glory in his strife?
    Is there meaning in his life?
Can God hold such a thing-like person dear?"

Thing-like person? So she may have seemed; but she was a King's messenger. She had been away from her village for some time, and now returned, very old, very stupid, very ignorant. She had never learned to read, and she had long ago forgotten or ceased to be able to tell any Bible story she had ever known. The very name of Jesus our Lord seems to have slipped from her; she only spoke of God, using a word she might have used if she had been a Hindu; but she remembered it meant Father. And this was the word she gave Mimosa, to whom every lightest syllable was a crumb from the loaf of life.

"He will never forsake you; He has never forsaken me. Meditate on Him and He will not forsake you. In heaven"—she used the word that means "release"—"there is no pain. To that good place He will take you. He will wonderfully lead you. In every least thing He will wonderfully lead you."

And she repeated this over, as the aged will, and said: "He who is God is your Father. He will wonderfully lead you, *in every least thing He will wonderfully lead you.*"

Soon afterwards she lost the little memory she had, and no one knew what her thoughts were. But "she heard the angels sing when she was dying."

One other help was given.

In Mimosa's village there was a room where the Christians worshiped, and in the same room the children of their families were taught by a loud-voiced teacher, who chanted his lessons in a singsong tone, caught up and echoed down the street by the children.

One day when Mimosa was passing she heard the verse being chanted.

"Do not rub on ashes,
　Do not offer matted hair to idols.
　The boast of the boaster is like the bite of the snake;
　When the Coming King arrives to judge,
　　excuses will not pass with Him."

It was rather a medley of words, tossed together more because of their Tamil sound than for mental affinity. The gist of it, however, caught her fancy, so the jostle of ideas did not matter. Siva's ashes, the matted, undressed hair of the devotee offered to the gods, the prideful boast that falls before the Coming King—a new name this—led straight to a new idea. Her Lord must be coming back to the world. That was the one arresting thought.

We can gather up the less than an infant's fistful of seed corn given to Mimosa. We can count the seeds, they were so few: there were nine. That God is; that He loves, guides, and, being the God of gods, is all-powerful; that He listens when we pray; that we may think of Him as a Father; and that "He who plants the tree will water it." That the Place of Release is much better than this world, for there is no pain there; and that the Lord who lived here before will come back. She had also heard that "sometime, at the last," there would be a judgment and excuses would not stand. But this event felt too remote to find much place in her theology.

Of her Savior as Christ crucified she knew nothing yet. In the few minutes she had been with us we could only begin to tell His story, and chiefly we spoke of Him as the Lord who loved her. But she had seen Him without knowing Him. "Who is the Lord, that I might believe on Him?" And before the Savior of the world had time to answer "It is He that talketh with thee," she was caught away. But what can hinder the pursuing power of the love of Christ? And who can measure the force of the life of a seed? Open one of earth's little seeds and find the plant that is to be, carved in polished ivory. See the packing of the nourishment required. See, and worship and adore.

Of all the stories we have touched since we came to India, hardly one has humbled us so much—as we thought of our faithless fears for little Mimosa—as this one. But hardly one has lifted us so high in adoration, and in wonder, and in awe.

Chapter Twelve

Backgrounds

ONE evening, while these things were happening to Mimosa, we at Dohnavur spent an hour with the polariscope just acquired for our microscope. Joyfully we tried the different combinations offered by polarizer, selenite, and mirror. Feathery crystal of barium platino-cyanide, like sprays of peacocks' feathers, fairy cornucopia from a fern, the little thorny marvel of a sole's scale—these and a score of others held us enchanted. Then as the blues and lilacs and violets and purples paled into something like the steel-blue of sheet lightning, we wanted the indigo of the thundercloud for background; and for those opalescent seashell colors that are like nothing earthly, but must be sought for in air and water, we wanted the beryl of the sea. And so it went on until we knew the perfect background for each delight. The difficulty was to get it.

We had just touched perfection with an exquisite blue against brown like the bark of a tree—except that polariscope colors are never flat but always, as it were, an atmosphere. The little spikes on the sole's scale were gleaming poniards, and iridescent lights played on the plated armor—not a pearly tint was lost—when one of the children, eagerly sharing this pleasure with us, moved the adjustments and lost the perfect foil.

We tried to recover it, but in vain. We did not know the laws of light well enough to find it. Or it may have been that the setting sun had dropped its cooler tones and was only all-red flame. Whatever the cause, till days afterwards (when we found it again) we thought of it as a kind of little, visible, lost chord—beautiful, elusive, within the fraction of a turn of a wheel but out of reach of our commanding. If only we had better known the laws of light, if only we could have stayed the going down of the sun, would we not have found it with a touch?

———

Mimosa stood alone among her people,
a woman charmed by a beauty she could not show them.

We all have our small and private windows which look out upon great matters. This little clear window did for us that day look out upon far fields. What if we could look through some heavenly polariscope and read, as perhaps the angels read, the meaning of the background for the colors of our lives? But then we would miss the blessing of those who do not see and yet believe.

It is difficult to imagine oneself stripped of all helps to faith, whether from the text of the Book itself or these its illuminated illustrations; but if this story is to be understood, and not merely taken at a run and forgotten, there must be some mental effort here. Mimosa stood alone among her people, a woman charmed by a beauty she could not show to them. Round her were the blazing streets, the little, hot houses, the curious, unsympathetic faces, the crowding work of life. But always it was as if One just out of sight were moving through those streets with her. What He did with her was good. Was He not all-powerful, so that He could direct everything? Had He not shown her by a thousand secret signs that she was loved? Would she, who was only a human mother, deny one good thing to her little son if she had the power to grant it? No more would He!

In this way, by the low-set stepping stones that lead across the stream that divides the material from the spiritual, she found herself in a place where nothing could shake her. The strange colors of her background could not perplex her. And this was what she really meant when she said, not asking for blue days, but looking up steadfastly into grey skies, beaten by rain and wind, "I am not offended with You"—no, not even while her poor husband lay mentally disturbed and blind, and the people pointed at her and said, "Did we not say *Parpom*?"

Chapter Thirteen

The Golden Pot that Had Manna

*T*HE nearest asylum was 500 miles away. It might as well have been 5,000. Before a patient can be admitted there, various preliminaries naturally are required. Of these Mimosa knew nothing, nor did she probably know there was such a place as an asylum in the world. She lived through those months with her sari in her hand (to use her own idiom), which was her simple way of telling of prayer without ceasing, in mute appeal and faith that help was on its way. She did not try to pierce the thick mystery that has baffled mankind since the beginning but accepted it, unintelligible as it was, as "well." She merely besought, earnestly, that her husband's reason might return; for without the control of reason, a blind man can be very terrible.

And gradually it returned, and his eyes became less darkened. "We had no help. No medicine did I know of, nor had I money to buy it. It was only our God's healing." And she sent a thank offering to the Christian church which knew nothing of her.

Nor did we in Dohnavur know anything of her. Through all these years Star and Mimosa had been kept apart. Never once had Mimosa been allowed to accompany the other sisters who sometimes came to see us; nor had Star been allowed to hear anything of her. Now, at last, she heard of her distress, and longed to get in touch with her. But how? Mimosa could not read. It was not likely that verbal messages would be given. After some pondering, Star decided to write. "O my living Lord, incline the heart of someone to read it to her," she prayed as she wrote, and believed it would be so.

And so it was. The letter safely reached Mimosa's house, and a kindly cousin read it to her.

---

*"Though my father and my mother may forsake me,
the Lord will draw me close to Himself."*

Trembling with joy, she listened. For Star had been constrained to write to her as to a fellow-believer and fellow-lover. Almost wondering at herself—for she could not understand why she was so directed—Star had applied the twenty-seventh psalm to this, as she thought, Hindu sister, copying in full the verse which in Tamil reads: "Though my father and my mother may forsake me, the Lord will draw me close to Himself."

Strange that what is "life of life" to one is mere dust of words to another. The cousin read indifferently in the singsong drone of India; as coined gold Mimosa received the words, loving them, desiring to linger over them. But coined gold is a poor simile, and, though little enough of it had come her way, Mimosa would have heaped it in handfuls on the floor for just those words that she heard now.

Then, the reading over, she took this, her very first

letter, in her hands, and touching her eyes with it in the pretty, reverent way of the East, she carefully folded it and put it in the box where she kept her one possession of value, the title deeds of her little house. If she had heard of the golden pot that had manna, that was kept in the Ark of the Covenant overlaid with gold, she would have thought thus of her precious letter. And thereafter when overwhelmed by troubles and sorely in need of sustenance, she would go to that box and take out her letter and, smoothing its pages with tender fingers, try to recall the words written upon them. Or if the friendly cousin could be found, she would get him to read it to her again, till, fed by that hidden manna, she was strong to continue. But it never occurred to the cousin to write and tell us about her, nor did it enter her mind that such a thing could be done. So we went on knowing nothing.

Chapter Fourteen

The Stab of a Knife

SLOWLY, very slowly, the months crawled past. Mimosa had to go to work or the food would have failed. So she combed her hair with her fingers (for after the birth of one's first child she is no longer allowed to dress her hair before going out, or to wear any dear little frivolous bell-bangles on arms and ankles) and she went to the fields and worked. Her husband lay like a log on his mat and was one more to feed. Kinglet could be trusted to attend to his own needs, and when she could not take them with her he would watch over Mayil and Music.

"Go first and see Mayil! Go first and see Mayil!"

One day Mimosa's brothers came to see their elder sister, a widow who lived nearby, and they took little Mayil to spend the day with them.

In the evening when Mimosa returned from the fields and was starting as usual to prepare the evening meal, deep in her heart, "just here"—and she showed where the words cut—"pricking, pricking like the prick of the point of a knife," was this: "Go first and see to Mayil! Go first and see to Mayil!" And she obeyed. Flying across to the other house and breaking in upon the company gathered there, she found them playing cards. In a flash (as she recounts it) one sees the very gesture of the card players, the half-closed eyes, the swaying forms, hears the peculiar little sounds of the game, as she saw and as she heard them in that one unforgettable moment.

"Oh, you to play while my little peacock lies dying!" She flung her indignation at them and fled with her child stiff in convulsions in her arms.

What had happened she never found out. If it was known, no one told. For a fortnight Mayil lay at death's door, then slowly recovered and came back to her.

But he lay in mortal weakness, and the neighbors, moved by sight of her anxiety, urged her to offer a chicken and a few coconuts. "So little, does she begrudge so little?" They told her what would happen if she did not do it. Her child would die. They watched her then, as she knelt before her God, the God invisible, who was, she said, the only true God. But it must have been that He did not hear, or, hearing, did not care, for He did not come to her relief. He abode still in the same place where He was—that far, far place to which, as all who came assured her, prayers without gifts to further them could never find the way.

There was no doctor, of course; there is no mission hospital in this whole reach of country, no place of any kind where a little child would be sure of skilled care, no avenue of help that was not far beyond her means to secure. So little Mayil lay with his two fingers tucked into his mouth in his old baby way, thinking to comfort himself so; and his mother, with her very heart breaking for love of him, saw him slowly growing worse.

It was very hard for Mimosa to live without going to work. Several times during this illness she had had to leave him to get money to buy food. He had fretted sorely. If only he might quickly recover she would be able to take him with her. It was too dreadful to leave him and know he would pine for her all day.

And now comes what to some of us seems the most poignant page of this story. Mayil was recovering when a wise woman told his mother that, if only she gave him two duck's eggs chopped fine in water, he would immediately be well.

So, impressed by the wise woman's confident assurance, she bought two duck's eggs, boiled them hard, chopped them fine, mixed them with water, and fed Mayil, almost expecting to see the little thin limbs fatten visibly—so sure was the wise woman.

But at once he became very ill. Dysentery set in. Daily, hourly he grew worse.

Just then, while her husband still lay prostrate and her precious little son was so ill, the rain came on; the roof, unrepaired, leaked; and the mud walls fell in on the floor, all but on top of them.

How her husband was gotten out Mimosa does not remember. In the pouring rain she searched for shelter and found an empty house, but the rent asked was too high. Nearby was her widowed sister. That sister did not love her, for her ways were not hers. But, fearing the talk of the neighbors who would feel it too barbarous to refuse shelter under such circumstances, she opened her house to the family; and to her other labors Mimosa added the gradual repair of her home. Somehow she got a few palm leaves for the roof; bit by bit she gathered up the fallen mud and built it into place; but, before she had finished it, the shock of the disturbance and the chill had so acted on her little Mayil that even her eyes, that refused to see it, saw at last that he must go.

She took him in her arms. We who know her can see her as she did it. Never were tenderer mother-eyes, gentler, braver hands.

"My little one," she said, "listen. I have taught you to pray. Shall I pray now that you may be taken out of this pain? Let us pray to the Lord"—and she used the word her father had used in his dying hour, the Lord the Supreme. Then she prayed, and she said: "It is well, O Lord, whatever You do. It is well."

And Mayil said nothing, but lay with his two little fingers in his mouth. "These"—and she held up and touched her own as if they had been Mayil's—"it was the way he lay when he was a baby wanting me. And while he was sucking his fingers for comfort, the Lord took him."

Chapter Fifteen

Take Care of My Bird

CROWDS came, according to custom; few sympathized. Who could justly sympathize with a mother who had refused to save her child? The kindly women would abstain from reproach: but not all were kind, and the feeling of the place was against her. Had she not burned the tulasi? Had she not refused, even to bring sure health to the child, all magic, even the mildest—all efforts to appease the angry gods? She would not break a mere half-penny coconut in the devil's honor. What wonder gods and demons were ranged against her now!

"My child God gave; my child God has taken. It is well."

It is hard enough to bear grief when tenderness is all about one. What must it be to bear it when these pricking briars abound?

On the day he died the women, emboldened by the silence of her grief, said cruelly and openly to her that she, and she alone, was responsible; and they laughed at her vain prayers. "Was it that your God did not hear you? Or is it that you do not know how to pray?" And they pointed to the little dead child. "There lies your God's reply to you."

Then Mimosa broke her silence: "My child God gave; my child God has taken. It is well."

But she was weak and weary after the vain nursing, and she was ill with grieving; and when she was alone, and had not her God's good name to defend, the question would return, Why was not her little peacock left to her? Till at last it came to her that perhaps He knew that she, his poor mother, could not have taken proper care of so beautiful a child, "and so He took him to Himself that He might take better care of him." And she looked up with the old word: "I am not offended with You."

But long before this last comfort came, with the terrible hurry of the tropics his body had been snatched away from her. Sometimes—in cholera times, for example, when panic forbids the usual ceremonies—a man will pass from vigorous health through seizure, illness, death, and burial or cremation, within four hours. A child, with hardly a minute's pause for farewell, is wrapped in a little old cloth and carried out and burned.

"But my little one shall not be burned as a Hindu. As a child of the living God shall he be buried" had been her decision, and nothing would move her from it. She had no perfect sureness about him, for she did not feel that she could claim room for him in the Place of Release, the Christian's heaven, because he was not a Christian child, and yet she could not bear to seem to consign him to the uncertainty of his father's creed. "For myself I did not go to the church, so I was nothing, and had no right to ask for anything for him; and yet my heart insisted: 'He shall have Christian burial.'" So not a conch shell was blown for him. There was no wailing. And the little body was sown as a seed on the open plain, to wait the Resurrection of which his mother then knew nothing. And the people said: "She is mad. Who heeds what a mad woman does?" But Mimosa said: "My bird has flown." And she held up her hands with a gesture of committal. "Take care of my bird."

Chapter Sixteen

Hair Cutting

*B*ACK to her now recovering husband went Mimosa and continued her faithful nursing. His hair had not been cut for a year, or dressed in any way, or even once combed; for he would have felt a drop of oil or the touch of a comb to be as dangerous as water, which, as all know, is deadly in any kind of illness. Mats of hair lay about him in tangled heaps. But at last he was willing to have it cut.

But who would cut it? The barber was called and was afraid. It is unlucky to cut such hair. Mimosa took the scissors. "I will cut it. Let the ill luck be on me!" Her fingers were blistered before she had finished, but at last all was cut and carefully deposited on the dustheap. To burn it would have been too dangerous; the neighbors would have interfered. As it was, they were shocked. "What a wife!" they said, and turned up the palms of their hands at her.

But the barber did not mind, for he did not lose his fee; Mimosa gave it to him just as if he had done his work, a whole precious rupee. Are there any givers so generous as the very poor?

Chapter Seventeen

The Magic Medicine

YES, they were very poor now, and when the husband had recovered sufficiently to be able to do light work, Mimosa, who was by this time quite worn out and unable for the fields, urged him to accept it. He could see a little, and the work did not ask much of him; it was only to be traveling companion to a relative who was going to one of the holy places of the South.

It was beautiful there. The fresh wind blew through a gap in the hills; many pilgrims daily bathed under a great waterfall, believing that so they washed away their sins. Day by day heart-moving little scenes were staged under overhanging rocks and deep in the woods, by the water's edge and sometimes under the spray of the falls. Perhaps there is nothing in all the world of worship more heart-moving in its pathos than just this bathing of the body for the expiation of the sins of the soul.

Mimosa's husband bathed with the others, but he never thought of his real sins. They did not come within farthest reach of his consciousness. To him, as to all these bathers, *sin* was a word denoting ceremonial defilement: the touching of an outcast even in compassion and mercy, the involuntary contaminations of outward life—these, not what we mean by sin, still less his slackness and general selfish laziness, were what chiefly concerned him. Here and there there may have been one bather with a more enlightened sense—"one in a thousand, perhaps," said a pilgrim who sought far and had at last found forgiveness and cleansing and peace through Jesus Christ.

There was a wizard worshiping at the waterfall that year, and he gave Mimosa's husband a magic medicine. It was a black, inky, sticky substance wrapped in a leaf. Said the wizard: "Take a third portion of this medicine once a day for three successive days with a small part of the leaf. For forty days thereafter, take only food cooked in a new earthen vessel and served from the pot with a newly made wooden ladle. On the fortieth day, thy sight will be restored." And it was so. Mimosa's husband returned quite well!

India is the home of suggestion and of auto-suggestion.

Chapter Eighteen

———

The Talisman

WHEN he returned, he had much to say about the magical properties of that medicine. And Mimosa's neighbors had much to say to her.

"Poor foolish woman, have we not told thee that all thy troubles would pass if only thou wert wise as thy husband? Look at him, restored to health! And by whom? And by what? And thy little peacock, where is he? If only thou wert more wise, and hadst used good sense and followed our counsel, would he not be in thine arms now? O empty arms! O most foolish mother!"

"Who but a hard-hearted woman would refuse a charm to save her dying child? Did we not tell her, did we not say again and again: 'Follow the customs of thy country'?"

And so it went on until Mimosa was weary of it.

Reader, take note: People far wiser than she, men wiser than her husband, even wonderful, learned men who write many English letters after their names, have believed in charms and amulets and all such occult ways of securing good fortune.

It *was* true, and it *is* true. As this tale goes to press there has come by post a witness thereto in the shape of a green-covered ten-page brochure. It is promoting *The World-Renowned Talisman*. It contains a picture of the acclaimed object's inventor and one also of his imposing residence, with a temple alongside, as if in attendance on his house. And then comes a picture of believers coming for the talisman. And the pages are crammed with letters—not anonymous testimonials in the shamefaced manner of the West, but outspoken, explicit, and very interesting letters, signed and with the writers' addresses in full.

Here you see B.A.'s, judges and magistrates, lawyers and stationmasters, government officials and doctors and clergymen, and all manner of private people; also anxious students, or chiefly students relieved, for with the charm the stiffest examination becomes easy. All stand forward and with frank voices tell their happy stories. A surgeon "cannot find words imaginable to extol the inevitable effects of the charm. It is soothing balm to the afflicted minds of mankind who uses it." "My long-cherished desire of serving the Hon'ble the Maharajah Bahadur has been fulfilled. I am happy under His Highness' good esteem." This is from a High Court barrister-at-law with a tail ten letters long after his name! The *charm* did it! A police officer receives honors from the government, a student passes "under great difficulties" his law examinations, so does another his Cambridge Local—he stands first in his province—and an exultant B.A. writes of his thankfulness. But scores more attest its virtues in much the same language. "I proclaim [this] by beat of the drum," remarks one, for all are grateful, and have no false shame whatever. After all, why should they have any? What are examinations but trapdoors through which you crawl if you have luck, and in which you stick if you have not?

"I bought it for the purpose of passing the Matricula-

tion examination. No doubt through the wonderful efficacy I have gained a very brilliant result in it." "I passed
my Intermediate, which was hopeless to get through. I find
no words to express the efficacy of your renowned charm."

Businessmen rise rapidly and get large increase of pay.
Unfortunates involved in litigation win their cases. (What
if both sides wore it?) The charm wins in a huge lottery;
twenty thousand rupees fall into the lap of its wearer, whose
life it also "saves from drowning by its divine power. Even
my friend who gave me the talisman passed the Cambridge
Senior Local with four distinctions and first-class honors."

One thing she knew: If her God was the true God,
then He was over all.

As for the mysterious influences of the stars, they slink
away before it: "I suffered on account of bad effect of my
stars; I have been subjected to the evil effects of planets."
But the charm has ended that. It has been "working like a
galvanic battery. Its effect in guarding the evil influence of
planets is really wonderful. It bestowed on me good health
and happiness. It has increased the beauty and charming-
ness of my body." And the physician of two well-known
maharajahs (great kings) tells how the charm acts like a
spell. A tiny child just the age of Mimosa's little peacock
was saved from death through its means. And another says
simply: "I was unwell, and it did cure me. I do believe
there is something in it which prevents evil from doing
mischief." And so it goes on.

Having been brought up in an environment like this,

and knowing nothing whatever that did not breathe the same spirit, Mimosa pondered long. How piercing a thorn in the heart "if only" can be! "If only I had done this or that." Who does not know the pricking of that thorn? Could it be that she was wrong? Had she indeed slain, by her refusal to look this way at all, her precious little peacock? But she turned from the perplexity; there were many things that she could not understand. But one thing she knew: If her God was the true God, then He was over *all*. God *was* the true God, therefore He *was* over all. Therefore charms were *under* Him. And what need is there to go to the thing that is undermost when you may go direct to Him who is *higher* than all?

"Nay, shall I be as one who goes to the servant when he might go to the Master of the household?" Thus did she answer herself. "And about these matters, my Father, I do not know anything. But I think it must be enough to leave them with You, my Father." And she went on in peace.

Chapter Nineteen

In the House of Her Friends

AND at last with fresh courage Mimosa gained strength and set to work to retrieve her poor little fortune. In India, when one is sick, one's relatives come in clusters, stay a day or two, and depart, to return perhaps again if the sickness is prolonged. They come to inquire (so the saying is), to lament, and to advise. Not to do so would show lack of family affection and all proper feeling.

A death draws even larger clusters—the most distant relatives flock around then. And, as children always come with their parents and all must be fed, it may be imagined that illness and death are expensive luxuries and empty the family purse, unless it be a very full one, nearly as thoroughly as a wedding does. But no Indian householder would dream of omitting to provide food for all who come. At any cost it must be done.

The cost to Mimosa had been the sale of everything that could be sold; all went to feed her guests. She often went hungry herself. It was a lean time.

As soon as possible she got to work in the fields of the kind Boaz, but she looked (as she was) poor. No gold ornaments were in her ears, no necklet round her neck. The poorest in India, if of any respectable family, clings to this visible bank-deposit. To be in debt is nothing; you may be richly jeweled and yet be in debt. No one thinks anything of that, not even the creditor. You may even beg with jewels in your ears. The stoniest heart would not blame you or refuse you alms for any such trifling cause. But to be unjeweled is disgrace, humiliation, intolerable.

But Mimosa, as we know, had the most curious thoughts about such things. No one understood her. She was a law to herself. So she sold her few jewels kept back from the sale of her dowry and fed the flocks of kind inquirers, and did not go into debt. It was when she had none to wear that her brother's child died.

"Do not go to inquire," said her husband, for neither that brother nor his wife had come to inquire when her little peacock flew away, and for the moment she was sorely tempted to retaliate as her husband urged. But she put the thought aside as unkind, and she and her little sons went.

"Let us accept even this. Without the allowing of our God, it could not have been done."

The feast was spread; to each guest was given a large fresh leaf of young green plantain, like fine satin in texture, most beautiful of plates. On it was heaped rice with the various curries. The leaf once used is thrown on the ash heap, never used again.

When the one who was serving came to the unjeweled Mimosa and her two little sons, she laid before her an old leaf used by another guest, and on it was the rice and curry left over from that other meal.

Mimosa could hardly believe she saw rightly. No such

indignity had she ever before seen, heard of, or imagined. To touch the leaf of another is to become ceremonially unclean; to touch the food left over an unthinkable defilement. No child would offer such an insult to its fellow. To offer it to a guest—Mimosa was stunned, and sat silent. Similar leaves were put before her little boys. They understood the offence and burst into angry tears.

Then their mother knew what she must do. "Do not cry, my little ones," she whispered, and gently touched the indignant children, who would have risen and left the house. "See, we must be patient, we must be quiet. Say nothing to disturb the feast but take the food." And in a lower whisper she added: "Let us accept even this. Without the allowing of our God, it could not have been done."

But it cut deep. As soon as possible without causing scandal, she left the house; and, not trusting herself to accept food from friends on the way, lest her still hot wrath should boil over and she should say words better left unspoken, she and her boys walked the fifteen miles home; and, after bathing comprehensively as if to wash off the very remembrance, they all had a meal together blessed by love and good manners; and the boys, still seething with wounded pride, were comforted.

But her husband could not refrain from a "Did I not say to thee, 'Better not go'?" and her heart echoed him feelingly. How much better not to have gone!

That night she fought out her battle alone.

Well she understood the meaning of this rudeness of all rudenesses. It was a public affront, unforgivable from an Indian point of view, unforgettable. It has no English parallel. To set before a guest at a public banquet an unwashed knife and fork and a plate with remains upon it would be discourteous enough. But this was more. The religious element poisoned it. Ceremonial uncleanness is abhorrent here. Over our poor Mimosa swept great waves of longing for her little Mayil, the child they had not cared about enough to come to see her as he lay dying. And she had gone to them in their sorrow, meaning her very action to say: "I forgive you; let us be friends." They knew her going meant that, and this was their reply.

She thought of the two rupees they had refused to lend. That too she had forgiven. What was the use of forgiving? Stung through her very soul, she burned with shame as she lived through the day in the darkness of the night. Had they done it because she was known to be not as others were, but one who loved the Christians' God? But they were Christians. Why, then, this cruel affront?

Was it because she was unjeweled? She had not borrowed jewels to put in her ears (this would have been thought polite, but to her had not seemed honest).

Christians! Why were they so *different* from their God? Within five miles of her where she lay and wept was a true Christian man, pastor of the church, good to all and tender-hearted like his Master. And within that distance there were at least two or three Christian women who would have shown the Lord's love to her, if only she could have known them. But they were of another caste and had no access to hers, unless invited. And she knew nothing of them, nor they of her; for an unknown world may be in the house of our next neighbor, and five miles may contain an infinite distance. But Mimosa remembered the old woman who had been sent to her in her need. She at least had been as a very angel of God to her. Yes, but was this the guidance she had promised? *"In every least thing He will wonderfully guide you."* Had she been guided to that heartless house with its hateful outrage? And as she saw it and felt it again, hot shame scorched her. She had been flouted in her brother's house.

Why, oh why, were hearts allowed to be so unkind? Nothing that had ever happened to her hurt like this, and the barriers of her self-control, so painfully maintained through the morning and all through the day, having once broken down, left her to the mercy of heavy, sweeping waves of grief. "The waters compassed me about, the weeds were wrapped about my head." If she had known the words, they would have sounded through her then—in her longing for her child, her hurt at this rebuff, her loneliness of spirit among those who could not understand. And now, to add to her distress, she was conscious of the working of a new passion within. What about this flaming anger? Was anger right? Should she not forgive? But how could she forgive?

At last, and suddenly, she remembered her Lord.

"Remembering Thee, I straight forgot
What otherwhile had troubled me;
It was as if it all were not,
I only was aware of Thee.

"Of Thee, of Thee alone aware,
I rested me, I held me still;
The blessed thought of Thee, most Fair,
Banished the brooding sense of ill.

"And quietness around me fell . . ."

Oh, it is true, it is true. Whoso hath known that comforting can bear witness it is true. He who knew what it was to be wounded in the house of His friends; He who turned not His face from a shame which shames our hottest, reddest shame, making it feel cool and pale; He, though of all this she did not know, was with her then. The thought of Him brought Him near; just a thought and He was there, softening the sharp edges of the pain, soothing, tending, cooling, comforting, till her soul was hushed within her. She took heart to forgive, and she slept.

Chapter Twenty

The Fortunate Fourth

MIMOSA'S boys are full of character and very lovable. The eldest is a thoughtful, upright little lad; the boy who followed Mayil is a child of delicate spirit. Then comes the treasured fourth, whom, from the first minute we saw him, we called Mischief.

The fourth child, if a son, is supposed to bring good fortune to a family. The fifth, if a daughter, and the fourth, if a son, are the children of good luck. Woe betide a family in which the fourth child is a girl or the fifth a boy. Children of ill omen, cursed by the gods from their birth, they bring misfortune upon all who belong to them. Mimosa hardly let her Fortunate Fourth out of her sight, and in fact never parted from him for a day. He was the very light of her eyes.

The night before his birth she had been in sore trouble. Her husband had fever in a distant town, and she could not possibly go to him. In vain she had tried to think of ways of helping him. There was nothing she could do, and her heart failed her. It was one of her darkest hours; she could not see a light anywhere at all. She tried to pray, but no words came. She could only look up in the dark and say: "O Lord, O Lord!"

Then she fell asleep, and she dreamed that she saw her

babe, a boy, a child of good fortune. He was lying beside her on her mat—well, whole, and good to look upon. And as she looked and loved him, she saw a snake coil round him and then glide under the door of the room and out of the house into the street. And when she told her dream, all united in assuring her that it was most propitious. The snake was Saturn, god of ill luck. He had haunted her for many years—witness her tribulations, poverty, illness, the death of her little peacock. But now all would change. Had not Saturn departed?

And in the unaccountable way things happen here, immediately after the boy's birth her husband, for the first time in his unfortunate life, found a gold jewel lying on the open road and brought it straight to her. They waited a while and inquired for the owner; but she (it was a woman's jewel) could not be found. Then, feeling it was clearly theirs, they had it made into a necklet—a little bank, not very safe according to our ways of thinking, but always at hand, within sight, something visibly between oneself and nothing. Given in such a way, it was doubly valuable, and the husband was encouraged, and the salt bazaar prospered; and Mimosa, who had taken the gift from the God of gods and wore it gratefully, was happy too. Verily He was stronger than Saturn. If, indeed, the snake were that malevolent influence, was it not He who had caused it to depart?

Chapter Twenty-One

———

Mylo, the Bull that Went to Heaven

"AND soon after that the bull went to heaven."

She was telling me the story of her years in a gentle reminiscent way, and suddenly, with almost startling emphasis, fell this sentence: "The bull that went to heaven." Obviously she knew something about that pleasant place; she had heard about the lovely open gates and the walls whose foundations were jewels, and the bright streets, and the river and the trees. It is this picture of glory and beauty that first holds the imagination of the child and the child-like. Later conceptions can wait. Did she envision the golden pavement of those wide streets being trodden—as the streets of all towns and villages are here—by leisurely sauntering bulls, glorified probably to suit the place, but still the bulls she knew? And if there were a river and trees, there must be open country nearby, many spreading miles of it. Why, then, not bulls?

"Yes," she continued dreamily, as if living through that evening when her bull went to heaven. "Long, long ago, on a day of sorrow, I had gone to a field of my mother. In hunger of heart I went and in thirst, and the field was called the Land of Precious Water. For nearby there was water where the workers could go to drink, and always the cotton grew well there.

"In that field, in my thirst, I drank of precious water; not the water of earth, for there indeed my true God spoke to m̄e. The cotton was young then; it was the month after the sowing and the plants were a span high. I hung my baby's hammock to the branch of an acacia. It was covered with yellow flowers, such as always come, balls of sweet-smelling yellow. I see it all again.

"Now to me came that field for a year's use, and the salt bazaar prospered. We bought a pair of ploughing bulls, and one of them was grey and the other was brown. It was Mylo, the grey one, that God took to Himself.

Grace can enable us so to pass through things temporal
that we finally lose not the things eternal.

"But first, great had been our gain. These my hands weeded the field and tilled it. No idle coolies did I call; with my own hands I tended the plants and gathered the cotton and carded it. So all the gains were ours. And they were far larger than they had ever been before, so all the people wondered. And my husband said: 'The first spending must be for thy ear jewels.' So they were bought.

"Then one evening at dusk, for no reason that we knew, Mylo, the grey bull, turned from his food, and he lay down, and God took him.

"We grieved. So much had we meant to do. It was not a little loss to us. But what could a person do? He was gone.

"Then like a light upon me fell a thought. Must not all that the good God does be good for the child that is His? Is any ill permitted to approach? Then is not *this* good? What if Mylo the bull had lived? Might we not, perhaps, have gone on desiring and, adding field to field, become entangled in the love of earthly things?

"Then remembered I my husband's elder brother, the subtle one; gain to us could not be without ravenous thoughts awakening in him. Family feuds would have arisen. We would have become enmeshed in new varieties of distresses. This foreseeing, had not my God, as a Father going in the way before His children, cleared a path for our feet, lest they should hereafter be caught in the net?

"Thus Mylo, the bull that went to heaven, was to us a bull of blessing, not to be mourned over but accepted with tranquility. And, wondering at the wise ways of my God, I remembered the saying of the old grandmother: 'You will be wonderfully led. *In every least thing you will be wonderfully led.*'"

It was not so difficult for her husband. He took it as his fate, and Fate had never been very kind to him. And this talk of his wife, though curious, was comfortable to his ear; for, after all, eventually fields meant exertion, and exertion was undesirable. Now they could be quiet. But for the wife, with her sense of capacity and keen, adventurous spirit, it was a real trial at first, and this thought was, as she said, like a light. She knew nothing then of that particular provision of grace that can enable us so to pass through things temporal that we finally lose not the things eternal. So the thought came with a new composing force, and ever after she looked back lovingly on Mylo, the little grey bull that went to heaven, marking a track for them all, as it were, with his four little hoofs.

Chapter Twenty-Two

Siva's Sign

*B*UT would they follow it? Kinglet, her first-born son, had rubbed Siva's ashes on his forehead.

Some distance from Mimosa's village is a celebrated town which is a very fort of Hinduism. Its temple dominates it from center to rim; things are done within its walls which could never be written in a book. "Sodom? This is Sodom," said one who knew. In this town Mimosa's husband was now living with his disreputable brother, and he took his eldest boy to live with him there. Nothing Mimosa could do could prevent it. The man was stubborn now with the set will of the weak.

Among his friends was a rich merchant who wanted a little boy to train as helper in the bazaar. Kinglet was to be that little boy. But first he must behave as a proper Hindu should. He must rub Siva's sign on his forehead. So his father took him to the temple.

The temple in that town is a gigantic place. Great pillared corridors, with sculptured columns and carved stone roofs, and awful chambers with doors that look as if all the powers that ever were could not move them on their hinges. In the glare of daylight it is overwhelming enough; at night it is stupendous. It was night when the father took his son, led him in through the mighty doors past which only certain castes may go, on to the far end of the darkness, where a hundred lights twinkled around the inmost shrine.

And there he told the boy to rub on Siva's ashes, the *Vibuthi* that his dying grandfather had refused. To do so would mark him a worshiper of Siva.

Kinglet thought of his mother and shook his head and tried to push away the ashes. But what could a boy do against those tremendous influences? His father "smote him with his words." The glimmering darkness did the rest. He yielded, and the ashes were rubbed on for the first time, and thereafter daily. Siva had won.

And Mimosa heard of it. She went alone to her little room of refuge. "O my Father, can I bear it? Will all end wrongly? It seems so, my Father. I cannot understand it. I prayed for something quite different. Will not my prayer be answered?" And her tears fell as they had never fallen even when Mayil was taken; for this was a piteous thing and bitterer than death. It was torture. Even now, long afterwards, when her boy's brow is washed clear, she can hardly speak of it. Her very soul quivers at the memory of it.

And then—and she does not know how to tell of its coming; she only knows it came—peace once more filled her heart. "I will not trouble You with more askings," she said aloud. (All her communings with her Father were aloud, except when sorrow or gladness passed beyond the reach of words.) "I will leave all I have asked with You. Is it not Your concern? Have You not heretofore most wonderfully led me? In every least thing have You not led me? Was not that word that was spoken to me true? Then why do I grieve like this now? I and mine, my husband and my children, I think, Father, are Your care. Is it not so? Then I need not be afraid." Perhaps the triumph of faith is too full-toned a word for such an experience. But did it not come near it?

And after that she rejoiced in any good thing she heard about her little son; for example, that he was the one boy the merchant had found who was perfectly honest in word and deed. "I had said to my Father, 'Let that be so; let there be given to my children a perfect truthfulness.' This virtue He had given to Kinglet. The merchant sold many things—coconuts and oils of all kinds, and spices and fruits; but he could leave the bazaar to my boy and knew all would be right when he returned. The money taken he could trust with him. When Kinglet left him he wept—yea, wept—for he said: 'Not another such shall I ever find.'"

It was a sweet cupful of joy; but the one drop of poison in the cup was the sight of the ashes on her boy's forehead when he came back, as he did twice a year for five days, to see her. She would rub the ashes off—she could do that—but she could not keep them from being rubbed on again, and all that was connoted by that one single sign was grief and abhorrence to her. For she had kept him pure from taint of idolatry from his babyhood. And he was her first-born son.

Chapter Twenty-Three

The Unlucky Fifth

AND now crashed down on her a blow; nothing she could do could ward it off from herself and her beloved. Her fifth child was a boy.

The neighbors came to see. They compassed her about like bees. They pitied her, they blamed, according to their various dispositions; they wagged their heads and turned up the palms of their hands; and they prophesied terrible things.

Poor Mimosa, she was not wiser than her generation. Had she not seen disaster follow upon the birth of her elder sister's fifth child (who was a boy)? And had not prosperity attended her own family in the years following Star's birth? For Star was a fifth child, a daughter of good fortune. To go no farther than her own household, had not the finding of the jewel and the blessing on the field followed the birth of her fourth, the Fortunate Fourth?

She listened now, downcast, unable to escape from the feeling that she had failed them all; vague fears haunted her; she had no word of excuse or of explanation for her fault.

"Let him perish. It is the only suitable thing to do."

"Give him away. Get rid of the danger. Give him away!"
For there are those in India who welcome such gifts and

train them for their own purposes.

"Kill him!" There is a cactus hedge outside that village where such children may be laid. The crows find them and then the village dogs.

But Mimosa, true mother in every instinct, could bear no more. "Let my baby perish? Give him to a stranger? Kill him?" And her voice rose at every question. "Depart from me, ye women! Be he ever so deadly a child of ill luck, he is my true God's gift to me." And she snatched the baby from reach of their eyes and held him close to her breast. "Go, go, go; and come." And she would have none of them.

And after they had gone, lamenting and threatening, and explicitly announcing their opinion of her, his poor fool-mother, she turned to her God. Their *Aiyo*s and *Aiyaiyo*s deafened her ears, distracted her soul, for every kind of dreadful emotion can be crammed into that expletive. She could not speak for a while. And then at last she found words, and she prayed that her despised fifth might grow in strength and in beauty. So that all must see he was fair to God. The more they terrified her with their forebodings, the more beautiful might he be. Oh, that they might be compelled to admit her God was stronger than all the gods, even the gods of ill luck—even Saturn, if indeed he had returned.

She gave him no name. What name could she give to such a son? All Indian names have known meanings, and a Tamil will change a letter in a word rather than use it unsuitably. *L* is a letter for feminine name endings, *N* for masculine. When a Christian wants to call his offspring The Sorrows of Mary, if the child be a girl, then the word for the Madonna is Marial; if a boy, Marian. With the usual careful regard for the suitable, Mimosa, not finding it, waited. But when, later on, we suggested Gift of God, she was delighted. That was exactly it.

Her prayer was answered, and the boy grew strong and fair. He could sit up alone at six months, and never ailed for an hour. Then measles came to the village, and measles is to India what smallpox is to England. All four boys sickened, her jewel child nearly died, and the baby boy lay in her arms a little bundle of bones.

Would it have been surprising if her faith had failed? Her husband, though restored to sense and sight, was entirely without regard for her distress, and he never took the least interest in her precious little fifth. She had not money to buy the remedies prescribed by the barber who doctored the village, and, what was much more serious, could not buy the extra nourishment required by the poor little fellows to fortify them to fight their illness, and they got weaker and weaker. Kept at home as she was now, she had even less money than usual.

The temptation to give up the faith that seemed to have failed and to resort to the ways of those about her must have been tremendous through those weeks. There were the demons of disease to be appeased, and that vindictive god of ill luck. "Only a coconut and a few flowers! Was it much to give to win health again for the poor sick children?" said the voices around her again; and again they urged charms to be bought or found. One, sinless and inexpensive, a frog which, if tied in a bag round the neck of the sick and starved to death, gives its slowly departing strength to the sufferer, at least should be tried. There were many workers in magic among the people of the village. They had ways of winning help. Mimosa never doubted that. Nor can one who has been among them doubt it either; think of the Egyptians: "They also did in like manner with their enchantments." There are no obsolete words in the Book written for all time. Call the strange powers exercised by those who give themselves to evil by any name you will, those powers exist.

Mimosa knew where to turn for help—at a price. But she would not pay that price, so she was bombarded again by the ceaseless chatter of the women: "Return to thine own gods, and will not thy troubles cease?"

"Fear not, O thou fool-woman, the gods are merciful. Offer the appointed sacrifice and all will yet be well."

"What hinders thee? See, thy days are as the surface of the water that is stricken by the wind. Wave after wave come thy distresses; they chase one another. So it must be with those who despise the ancient gods."

"And thy father, art thou better than he? Or wiser? Did he forsake the gods of his people? Did he not hear the foreign talk and refuse it? Art thou superior to thy father?" For that by his last words he had confessed a faith till then hardly known to himself had never occurred to anyone.

"See her, the wisdomless!" they would continue relentlessly. And harder words came at call, and they pushed her and struck at her and trampled her down.

And she was as sensitive as the mimosa by the roadside that the cattle tread down on their way home in the evening. A breath, and a tremor runs through the little thing; it can feel even the changes in the air caused by thunder. Touch it, and one by one the leaflets close, each pinna droops and the leaf-stalk drops with a jerk. Only the pretty lilac balls look up to the sun. "It is dead," says the child who sees it thus for the first time; but it is not. By the ditch where it grows, there is a trickle of water from the rice fields. Nourished by this it takes heart again and shows its delicate bravery, as if nothing rougher than the flicker of a butterfly's wings were in the world at all.

Succor came to our human Mimosa. The secret hidden waters flowed about her roots and, like her namesake by the roadside, she took heart to live again. The very trials that befell her were turned to means of strength for her; by them she proved her Father. For "if the work be of God, He can make a stepping stone of the devil himself to set forward the work."

All four boys recovered. "By my God was their healing," she said in speaking of it afterwards. "By Him alone it came, for none of the things I would have done for them was I at that time able to do." And, moved by the love which cannot rest without giving, unconcerned by questions about how the Lord of all the universe could care to receive her trivial gifts, she sent part of her first earnings, by the hand of her little boys, to the church.

Chapter Twenty-Four

The Ceremony of the Corner

"THY father, art thou better than he? Or wiser?"
She had refused the word when they flung it at her,
but it rankled like a thorn in her soul, and again and again
she felt the hurt of it. And one day, pitifully lonely, she
seemed to walk back through the years to the hour when
she first realized her father had indeed gone, never to return.

It was just eleven days after his death, and the Cer-
emony of the Corner had begun. She saw it now, felt it,
lived in it, was part of it again.

• • • • •

The doors and windows of the long, low living room
are shut. The air is heavy with a smothered smell of frankincense. There, in the dimly lighted corner, is her father's
muslin scarf outspread. On it she sees his little, dear, own
things, his brass betel box, his betel nut parer, and a morsel of lime. She sees his books too, some of paper, some of
palm leaf strung in a frame. His gold rings are there, and
his silver waistchain, his sandals and umbrella. Is that not
his step in the house? Will he not open the door and come
in?

But no, it is only women who are coming. Mimosa
sees them, all her women relatives to uttermost degree; for

this is the Women's Festival; no man comes near it.

Now the room is full to the doors. It is very hot and stuffy. Each woman has a leaf in her hand.

The doors are opening. Pressing through the throng come Mimosa's elder sisters. They are spreading the feast for the dead. Rice cakes, piles of knobbly sugarballs, curly honey cakes, slabs of sticky, luscious gum, nutty lumps of moist sugar. All except the rice cakes are oily. Mimosa smells the oily smells. Sesame and coconut mix with the castor oil that feeds the wicks afloat in shallow cups in the tall brass lamp. Through these mixed smells come little whiffs of frankincense.

Now by the flickering yellow light Mimosa sees the women gather in a tight knot around the white scarf in the corner. They are looking at the little intimate things, and their hearts are moved.

Mimosa is crying quietly. The sandals and umbrella— why does he not need them for this journey? Where has he gone?

Now one takes a censer and burns sweet spices in it, and drops incense on the flame, and slowly "censes" the offerings. And each woman shakes down her hair and, dipping her leaf into the incense, lights a morsel of camphor and touches her brow and breast and eyes with the ashes. And she marks, each woman on her forehead, Siva's sign.

And they chant the death dirge, swaying backwards and forwards till they are exhausted.

Mimosa, tears falling fast, hair in masses down her back, sways with them, chants the death dirge too, cries to the father perhaps not yet out of reach.

Then, with a quick change of feeling, the women spring

up, and Mimosa with them, dazed as she is and startled; with them she twists up her hair in a deft knot, picks up a fragment of sweet or cake, goes out with the others to the courtyard.

Now the clear blue is above them, and about them the usual things of the day. They toss their sweet things in the air, and call *Ka, ka!* and the crows flock down pleased and noisy and commonplace, and the wild frenzy of a moment ago is as a dream when one awakes.

A little apart Mimosa stands, dazzled by the bright light and the noise and the crows' clamor. And her mother pours into each outstretched sari handfuls of the good things from that scarf in the corner, and the Ritual of the Corner is over.

• • • • •

Mimosa drew a deep breath. Why had she been so long away? She shook herself impatiently; the day's work must be done, she must come back to it. But still she stood among the shadows. The spell of the drone of the dirge was upon her. She was breathing still the heavy air, smelling the incense and the oils, seeing through the bluish smoke the flicker of yellow light, the white cloth, the brown and golden cakes and sweets, and the dear familiar things, feeling the clutch of them at her heart. Drugged by the scent of the frankincense, she was one of those swaying women still, chanting the dirge of the dead.

As one writes, one is there oneself. Such experiences are unforgettable. Where there is real sorrow, it is as if love, longing, a wistful wonder, pity, sympathy, and almost awe and fear—for the things of the dead bring him almost back—like so many strings of a delicate instrument, lie exposed for the play of unseen fingers. The women seem to spread their very being bare to the influences of emotion. And then the dramatic change, the sudden releasing of a too taut string, the run out into the open and the light-hearted tossing of the food to the vociferous crows, the simple, sensible turning from the clouded mysteries of death and grief to the commonplace of pleasant food—who that has shared it could forget? Back to their homes the women go, laden with sweets for the children there, and all is good and normal again. Only the sorely bereaved mourn still. For them the pain is a devouring thing that cannot be appeased.

But of the meaning of it all they hardly seem to think. No one troubles to tell them that the throwing of food to the birds, like the laying of a ball of rice on the dead mouth, is for the nourishment of the subtle body which is all that now remains between the departed and absorption in the universal soul. All the women know is that somehow the dead are helped, for a faith in life after death continues imperishable in the human heart, and they trust their dead live somewhere. But Mimosa, coming slowly back from that hour of memories, longed to know more, to be sure; ached in every fibre for her father; above all, yearned, *burned* with desire to know if indeed he had turned to her own true God at last. He had passed with only that one unexplained word: "I go to the Supreme."

Could it be that he had accepted the truth, though at the very threshold of death? "O father," she had almost cried, and then stopped, knowing nothing of any such appeal, and turning to the ever-living Father she rested her heart on the knowledge of a love that she had proved and could lay hold upon, undismayed by unanswered questions. "You know all these matters, my Father; to You are not all such things perfectly known? And as for me, I cannot leave You. No, not even if my own mortal father did not know You, can I leave You. You are known to me, my Father. And will You not take care of us, these my children and me?"

Chapter Twenty-Five

The Empty Oil Bottle

SHE was not through her troubles. That treacherous illness had left weakness in its wake. An infection of the skin attacked all four boys; the poor baby was covered with sores and wailed day and night. Lavish anointing with oil would have helped, but the oil bottle was empty, and she could not afford to buy in anything like sufficient quantity.

That was a painful hour. She could have borrowed the oil, but the strange instinct in her, uncommunicated by anything ever heard (and, as we know, she could not read) drew her back from borrowing. "Our God knows, and He will give it to us. He will help me to earn more, give me more strength. If it be good for us, this He will do," she said to her little boys.

But that night, as she saw the poor little fellows distressed and crying, she must have been sharply tempted. Ever since they were born, she had sent thank offerings by one of the children to the God of the Christians whom she also worshiped. Sometimes the gift was a small silver coin, sometimes a handful of salt—firstfruits, as it were, of the season. The child laid it on the tray set for such gifts and came away, no one inquiring. Never had anyone thought anything of these gifts; they were not published in any list. They went into some general fund, unnoticed, except that sometimes somebody would remark in a dim, wondering kind of way: "Why does this heathen woman send offerings to our church?"

But now all was different. If a trifle of these often hardly-spared gifts had been kept back, the children would not be crying now. The poor mother pulled herself together. Such thoughts must never enter. She went to the little boys, made them kneel on their mats: "Our God can help even in this," she said, and she prayed—prayed for healing, for relief from the unendurable irritation which kept them awake, for help for herself that she might be strong to work and buy what was required, for comfort for them all. Soothed and consoled, the children fell asleep.

But the oil?

Through all these years her sisters had never thought of sending her anything. It was partly, perhaps, that they lived far away and knew little of her struggles; partly, it may be, they knew the temper of her mind and did not care to risk sending an unwelcome gift. She, of course, had never spoken of her difficulties to them; if they knew any-thing, they heard it from others.

For Mimosa, careful of her God's good name, said noth-ing to those who would not understand. "I know His love; how could I doubt Him? But if I had told them they would have said, 'Ah, your God is not so good as ours. See, we lack nothing.'"

But now, in their distant town, to the two sisters came a thought of Mimosa and her children, and moved by some kindly, sisterly feeling, they sent twice during that period small, but blessedly welcome gifts. (For so coming, who could refuse them?) The oil bottle was filled, and there was enough to buy other necessities of the moment. Cheered and warmed to the heart (but she would have said *cooled*), Mimosa thanked God and took courage.

And in this way, by prayer and in confidence, this un-taught Indian woman dealt with all the emergencies of life, taking sickness, when it came, direct to Him, and look-ing to Him to heal. She never seems to have worried over petty questions about the use of means. She would have opened her brown eyes wide with wonder had anyone sug-gested that the good eucalyptus oil which can take the pain from a scorpion sting within one minute was less a gift of her kind Father than the rice was, and the vegetable curry which nourished her little sons.

In a world where she had never walked, Christians were thinking and writing about healing in answer to prayer. Of all this, of course, Mimosa had not heard the lightest whisper, nor had she heard a single story of the healing virtue of our Lord. But, taught by the Spirit, she was led straight to the heart of the matter. To her faith, unperplexed by the talk of men, it seemed a natural thing that He should heal. And, though relief did not always come at once, peace did. "And is not peace of more importance?" she said in her sweet simplicity.

When asked to explain why some did not recover— her little Mayil, for example—she turned tranquil eyes upon the questioner. She did not know; but her God did. So must it not be well? And that was her answer continu-ally about many puzzling matters. With a turn of the hands which, in Tamil, talk as much as the tongue, and a smile that illuminates her otherwise serious face, she says it now.

Or she glances up with a quick "Father, You know. It is well, I think, Father; it is certainly well."

Does it read like a story made up, or at least touched up a little? But I have never consciously written an untrue line, and a story, even ever so little colored, would be untrue.

And is there any need, even if it were allowed, to invent or to color where the truth of God is concerned? Are not His doings, shown just as they are, quite beautiful? "Impossible" things are continually happening, for He has not gone away from His world.

Chapter Twenty-Six

Redeemer, Christ, Command Thy Double Healing

NOR has He left Himself without witnesses. Mimosa's village is well known to the police. The District Superintendent of Police once told us that there was more crime there and round about that village than anywhere else in the district. He told us stories such as only such men can tell, stories that would make weird books if anyone had time to write them. And in the thick of this lived Mimosa and her children. But in that clan, thus notorious for every kind of daredevilry, was the gentle cousin who had read Star's letter to Mimosa. No one had ever heard him say a rough word, and round about him there was a little quiet place always.

And it was he who, time and again, was a witness to the universal love of God whose poor children had forgotten Him and were becoming so terribly like the gods that they had fashioned.

One day Mimosa, who had been slowly failing for some time, became very ill. Somehow she struggled through the cooking of a kind of food that would keep good for nearly three days. She had hardly got it made when she collapsed, and for three days she lay helpless. No one knew, and no one came to see her. Her frightened little boys kept close to their poor mother, not understanding what was the matter, and, when mealtimes came, they took the food she had prepared prior to becoming too ill to move. But she had nothing. She could not eat.

And she could not rise and spread her sari to the Lord; but that was her spiritual attitude. Her *soul* knelt.

"Send help, I ask You, Father. I am sure You know how things are with me. And You know how I should get up and look after my children. But see, I cannot get up. The pain holds me down. Kindly allay it, Father. This is what I ask You to do, that I may rise and look after my children and the house."

On the third day a neighbor looked in and gave the alarm. Mimosa seemed to her eyes to be dying. She had the dreaded death-delirium. "She is dying, she is dying!" she cried, rushing out into the street.

And her cousin, the man of quietness, heard. Quickly he ran for a vessel of oil and, going straight to her where she lay, began to anoint her with it, rubbing her gently in the Indian way. And to the amazement of the people who by this time had gathered for the last scene, she sat up.

Then her cousin went for food and fed her children, who had just begun to be hungry, and to her he gave the rice-water given in illness; but she was soon ready for proper food, for "healing had come, even health. I had no pain and soon was strong again."

And she told me how astonished the people were; but to her sweet and simple faith it was not wonderful so much as kind.

When she came to us—for that joy is only a few chapters ahead—she lighted upon a time of new experiences with us, of healings given in answer to prayer such as we had not had before in the same definite and public way.

A hymn sung at these meetings has a chorus which runs thus:

> "Touch them, O Lord,
> Touch them, O Lord,
> We kneel and pray Thee, touch them,
> Oh, touch them, Lord."

And it goes on:

> "Redeemer, Christ, command Thy double
>   healing:
> For soul and body in Thy sight are dear."

At a time of preparation for one of these meetings Mimosa sat with her calm, fixed gaze on the speaker. There was such a look of comprehension in her face that it was as if she had been through it all before. And this though she was only just beginning to learn what our five-year-old children "had known ever since they were quite little," as one of them remarked. "She cannot even say the twenty-third psalm off by heart," said another, astonished. It was true. She had lingered for days brooding over the first two verses, which seemed to her so beautiful that she could not hurry to go past them. And yet, veriest babe as she was in knowledge of the letter of Scripture, she seemed to have drunk very deep of its spirit, and here she was meeting us more than halfway in this, as in everything else. So the one who was speaking asked her if she would sometime tell what she knew of our Lord Jesus Christ as Healer.

She smiled, and the smile that filled her grave eyes was like a glint of light on a mountain pool. And, sitting by the well the next evening while the children washed their saris, she told me the story just written down, feeling it would make it easier to tell it "in the great congregation" if she told it first alone in the quiet like this.

But the joy of her heart was not only, or chiefly, in the healing of the body experienced in her village home, or seen now. It lay, it lies, in the blessed truth that the Lord, coming thus near to a company of His children, does, in a way impossible to describe to those who have not known it, convey a new, fresh sense of His presence and His love and His power to those thus brought into contact with Him. Mimosa had heard her son (him on whose brow Siva's ashes were rubbed) ask her: "And is it really true? Will He heal my soul as He has healed these children's bodies?" He had seen the one done; he was awakened to believe in the other.

It was this that filled his mother's eyes that evening with a light that cannot be expressed in terms of earth's poor lights. It was starlight, moonlight, dawn, all in one; it was heaven's light we saw in her dark eyes then.

Chapter Twenty-Seven

The Fears of Love

*D*O LOVE and fear always walk up and down together in a mother's heart? Mimosa never knew what it was to be without fear for her little sons. She knew the perils of an Indian street; thick as the dust on it, those perils lay about her boys. She could not forget the indelible impressions etched deep upon the mind of a young child by the sights and the sounds of the streets.

Far back in memory lay a dreadful day when her father found his eldest son bringing into his own clean house boys with minds that were open sewers. He seized the wretched youth, tied him to a pillar in an upper room, and scourged him with a rope. Then, in his desperation, he did the most extreme thing known to Hindu fathers in the way of punishment. (It is meted out sometimes to lads who want to follow Christ and have confessed at home.) He put pepper in his eyes.

But vain, vain is all without the power of the cleansing Spirit to deal with the heart within. The boy was forbidden the privileges of the house, so his mother and sisters saw little of him. The father wrestled alone with his trouble. Yes, his son had wasted his property, but that was nothing to this; and when at last the abject one declared his intention of joining the Way, his father smiled a grim smile; the

Church was welcome to him.

The boy arrived at our bungalow on the Iyer's birthday. Not a hint of his past was allowed to filter through to us; nor was his motive—desire for education for commercial reasons—discoverable at once. He was received as a birthday gift from heaven, a new opportunity; with joy and with love he was welcomed; and he lived to make more scars in hearts that had trusted him and toiled for him. Such are the griefs of the angels, the shame of Christ. This boy, a man now, was back in his village, and he stung Mimosa with wasp stings of sharp words whenever he had the chance.

But she did not mind that, if only she could keep her boys from him and such as he. So she watched over them, combining that vigilant mother-duty with all else that she did.

They were almost always with her; for there was no one who felt as she did with whom she could leave them. They helped her with her housework, though that was against custom; for in India, boys are served, they do not serve.

At first they rather demurred.

"Buy a little sister for us," they said to her one day. "So-and-so and So-and-so"—naming boys of their acquaintance—"have little sisters who sweep the house for them and polish the brass vessels and help to cook. If we had one, we would not need to work at all."

Mimosa smiled. In her wise heart she felt it was no bad training, this unusual training of the house, and she told the little boys it was all right. They helped her so nicely she really did not need to buy a little sister.

Chapter Twenty-Eight

"Shall I Be Offended With You?"

*B*UT the children's long illness had drained her resources, and there came a night when once again there was no food to give them.

She remembered the refused two rupees. She would not risk man's rebuff again. "It will be enough, I think, if I tell my Father," was the word that lay deepest within her. But the noontide hour passed foodless; there was not a grain of rice or a single little green vegetable in the house. It was a time when it was impossible for her to go out to work.

She drew her little sons beside her. She had taught them that their Father would never forsake them. She had taught them to pray; from their babyhood they had knelt with her on their mats and followed her simple petitions. She had taught them to thank God before food, in the Christian way, for she had, in that one afternoon long ago, seen her sister do so. "We have praised our God when we had food," she said to the boys as they looked up hungrily and rather tearfully. "Now let us praise Him when we have none."

Then they knelt together. "O God, O true God, O Father, we worship You, we praise You." And she asked that contentment might be given to them, and sleep.

The boys lay down, and they fell asleep; but the mother could not sleep. Hour after hour she knelt before her God, holding out her sari in the old way, and, remembering her father's proverb, these were the words she said:

"If the gardener has to water a great many plants, will he not sometimes forget one little plant? My children and I are Your plants. You have the whole world to look after; I think perhaps You have forgotten us tonight. But never mind. (The word is half apologetic. Who am I that I should mention it?) Shall I be offended with You? Only I ask You to be as the hen with her little chickens. Gather us under Your wings."

It was now near midnight. The house was far too poor to keep a light burning: the little boys had prayed in the dark, and gone to sleep in the dark; and these words and many more—for she knelt there for a long time—were spoken in the dark. The darkness is full of demons to the people of the South. In cholera time I have gone down the unlighted streets of the village of Dohnavur, tapping at the doors of the houses where the worst cases lay, and I have never known a door to open without a cautious minute of frightened question from the inside. "We were afraid of the demons," would be the apology as at last the door opened and let me in.

Now through the dark streets, lighted only by the stars, came the sound of footsteps. They stopped at her door.

"Sister!"

She knew the voice and opened quickly. There, standing against the velvety star-sprinkled sky, she saw that same cousin who had been sent to her before. She had carefully kept the knowledge of her circumstances from him, for he was not a believer in her God.

"Hast thou any food? Have the children any food?" he asked.

What could she say? She knew her God had sent him, and throbs of joy shook her so that she could hardly speak. He had not forgotten; the Gardener had not forgotten His little plants.

But His honor was concerned in this matter, and she was very jealous for the honor of the Lord her God; so she hesitated for a moment.

"See," she said, pointing to the sleeping boys, as the starlight coming in through the door showed them on their mats. "We are happy. That is the chief thing, even more important than food. The children cried a little at first, but see, they are asleep. Our God has comforted them. Is not contentment more precious than food?"

But the cousin would not be denied.

Then she lighted a wick floating in a saucer of oil and woke the boys. In the yellow flicker those wondering children saw a brass vessel piled with white rice, and a joyful heap of the nice curried vegetables their little souls had yearned for set on the top of the heap. The cousin could not explain why he came. All he knew was that he could not go to sleep; something in him kept on wakening him and stirring him to take that food at once, till at last he yielded, went to the place where the rice left over from the evening's meal was kept, and, filling the brass vessel, brought it to them.

Chapter Twenty-Nine

"I Know Him by Suffering"

AND SO the last months passed before we were to meet. Her cousin was always kind to her. The rest of the world had only one word for her, and turned on her always the same hard face. But it grew more and more difficult to guard the boys; and, as they began to understand and ask questions, and the pains of a divided house became more insistent, all the mother-love in her burned in one pure flame of desire that they should have what she had never had, the chance to learn fully of the true and living and holy God and themselves choose His worship.

But how could it be accomplished?

She gave herself to prayer. Streaming through the busy day, flowing far into the night, it was not always in words, for such longings as consumed her cannot wait for words. "I am a prayer" might describe her.

This attitude could not be kept wholly hidden to her world, and one day her brother—he to whom so much had been given—taunted her thus:

"Thou thinkest that thou canst pray! From whom hast thou learned? Thou who canst not read, thou the ignorant who canst not even read the first letter (and he named it mockingly), thou thinkest that thou canst pray!" And he sniffed.

She turned her wistful eyes upon him. He knew so much. If he would only teach her! But such a thought was far from him.

She was only a poor woman, she said humbly to her-self; she knew nothing at all. What if this that her learned brother said was true? What if her concept was all a mis-take? Sharply and deep the sword entered into her soul. That miserable brother had thrust it again, twisting it around with malicious intent as his laugh rang down the street.

"You know Him by learning, but I know Him by suffering."

"Wilt Thou be indeed to me as waters that fail?" Did her heart cry that at this hour?

"I have prayed for thee, that thy faith fail not."

She had never heard the words, knew nothing of the truth that reinforces our fainting spirits. But wonderful, wonderful are the ways of the Lord. He is here, sometimes revealed to us, sometimes hidden, but always a God at hand and not a God far off. *Near* at that moment was the Lover of souls.

"Have I been a wilderness unto thee?"

Then with a warm glow of joy she knew what He had been to her all through the bitter years. "You know Him by learning," she later said to Star, "but I know Him by suffering."

It was a true word. She did not mean that Star knew Him by learning only, for Star has suffered too; but her reverent gaze was on Star's Bible and many books, and she knew that riches of knowledge lay in wonderful heaps in those rooms which she had never entered. "But I know Him by suffering." That poignant little word tells all.

No, He had not been a wilderness to her; He had comforted all her waste places. He understood that she had never learned to pray and did not know even the first letter of the Tamil alphabet, so had He not Himself taught her how to speak to Him, even as a mother teaches her little child? Then, as if to reassure her, He showed Himself again in another small, gentle act of kindness like that of the midnight meal.

Chapter Thirty

The Five Rupee Notes

NOT that Mimosa talked lightly on these matters. She seemed to have learned "to guard the inner wealth from the squandering of common talk." But when she discovered, to her joyful surprise, that His children here at Dohnavur were constantly proving His care even in these the ordinary needs of life, we met on common ground; and thus were drawn from her some of her own experiences to which we listened, wondering at the variety of our Lord's loving-kindnesses—what one might call the ingenuity of love.

And, wondering more, we recalled that single afternoon so many years before, with its medley of impressions: the excitement of her first look around a Christian house, the eager joy of being with her sister, the giving of that little fragment of truth with such a small hope on our part that so little could do anything—but oh, *imperishable* is every fragment of God's eternal truth!—and then the blinding grief of that closing ten minutes, which seemed as if it must have swept out of her mind that one little fragment. Who could have thought that anything planted in such a confusion and upturn of circumstances would have lived, and put forth roots, and grown, and budded as a rose growing by a brook of water? Who would have thought it possible? How could it have been possible but for the unimaginable lovingkindness of Jesus Christ our Lord?

And now, when things were hardest, came this new touch, as of a hand on her little affairs, that assured her of His presence. But *assured* is not the word. Have we a word for the incoming of that sweet sense of being taken care of, loved, not forgotten? Perhaps such sweetness passes earth's poor words.

The roof of Mimosa's house is made of palm leaves, and these require frequent renewal. If they are not renewed as soon as they begin to "go," the roof leaks. And a leaky roof is a very miserable thing. "Though one may stay in the house of sorrow, to be in a leaky house is impossible," says the proverb.

Hers needed repair. Five rupees (between six and seven shillings) would buy leaves enough to make all safe before the heavy rains of the northeast monsoon—rain that empties itself on these plains in solid sheets of grey water till life in our foolish South India is one great shiver. For we build for sunshine here, and improvidently forget rain and cold, except that in the matter of palm-leaf roofs we try to keep them watertight.

But food was dear, and the boys, who were growing fast, consumed a great deal of it. Food came first, roofs second; Mimosa could not spare that five rupees. And yet the roof must be repaired. She tried hard to earn more money, but she had touched her limit. Not another copper could she add to the day's incomings. But no one knew. "Only my God, He knew."

In the beautiful old Tuscany story, Sister Marianna, tired out after nursing a poor sick woman, fell asleep while the food she was cooking for her was still on the fire. But the Christ Child came and cared for that little pot of food, and it was not spoiled.

> "Oh, the Lord has many a way
> That His children little think of,
> To send answers when they pray.
> He had finished all she failed in."

Not in legend only, in real everyday commonplace life, these things are happening still. Only we do not always see the Christ or His holy angels in the house or in the street. Perhaps we forget to look for them. Perhaps this story is meant to be a witness to the invisible.

One day, while Music and Mischief (the Fortunate Fourth) were playing near the house, a wedding procession passed with a beautiful braying band and much shouting. After the dust had subsided, Music, who had been enjoying the mad racket to the full, saw some small pieces of paper lying in the middle of the village street.

In a house where letters never come—the one exception was that precious letter from Star, now stored away in the box—where there are no newspapers or pamphlets, paper has to be bought by the farthing's worth in the bazaar. The boy pounced on his treasure-trove; it would be just the thing for holding safely the sticky brown palm-sugar which from time to time his mother gave him for a treat.

But one of the pieces was dirty. He left it, and a less fastidious playfellow picked it up.

"Mother, mother!" he cried, running into the house. "Look at what I have found." And he suggested that she might keep the five little slips of nice stiff paper for his sugar.

His mother took the crisp little slips from him and noticed they were curiously cut and marked.

"This is not common paper," she said to the boy who waited eagerly; and remembering that she had heard talk of paper money, though she had never seen it, she wondered if this could be that, and took the slips to a neighbor. Each one was a rupee note! (The other carried off by her boy's playfellow was for two and a half rupees.) In her hand lay five rupees, the five rupees she wanted. Mimosa thought of her roof; but it might be possible to find the owner, so she waited.

Soon the story was noised abroad, and a man came to her door. Yes, her little boy had found the notes, she said, and she went to get them. But tender, tender are the mercies of the Lord. The man smiled and shook his head. "Let the little one keep them," he said, and went his way.

Thus continually, unfailingly, she was helped, and she went on in the quietness of a sure confidence. Was ever one less defended? But is it not to the city that has no moat or towers that the great word applies: "There the glorious Lord will be unto us a place of broad rivers and streams"?

Oh, the story loses sadly in the writing. First there is the poverty of bare words without any of the tender touches of the living telling. And then there is the loss of even what little those same poor words can capture, as they are hammered out in type and sewn up in a book. With every change of element something eludes one—floats away like a fragrance in the air, vanishes like color on the mountains when the living light of dawn passes into ordinary day. Often I have stopped and longed that this rare look into the life of an Indian woman might be given by means of some other sense than that of eye or ear. When shall we be able to *think* our tales across the sea?

Chapter Thirty-One

Star's Burden

AND now, away in Dohnavur, on Star—who was still unaware of all this—was laid a great burden of prayer. Mimosa and her little sons were never far from her mind. She longed to write to her and propose that she should come to see us. Over and over again she had all but written, and then "it was as if my hand were pulled back, like this," she said in speaking of it afterwards—and she laid her left hand on her right hand and held it, drawing it back. "I could not write, and I thought of Uzzah and the ark, and felt I must not touch this matter, which was not mine but belonged to God."

Then she began to pray that to the boys themselves the desire to come might be given (for the desires of little sons have a certain weight with their parents quite out of proportion to their importance). This prayer lay on her for three months, and then came four days of fever. She was shut up to prayer.

It was a strange experience. She earnestly wanted to be well, for there was no one to do what she had to leave undone. But it was as if one work only were given to her to do. She was to live with God for Mimosa. Gradually a great peace grew up in her heart, and, though the thought of her sister and her sister's children was with her all the time, the sense of burden was gone.

On the fifth day it was "as if the Lord Jesus came into the room." There was not the usual convalescence. She was at once quite well. He touched her hand, and the fever left her; and she arose and ministered.

Letters from her old home take a week to reach Dohnavur. Within a week from that fifth day when healing was granted, a letter came from Mimosa—the first Star had ever received from her. It had been written at different times during the four days of her fever.

What takes place in the spiritual realm when such things happen? How little we know of that which moves in and out of our ways and hems us in on every side.

Chapter Thirty-Two

Blockhead

BUT we must look back a little to see how by simplest means causes are set in motion that lead to answered prayer.

Down in the dusty, noisy world a boy of fourteen sat in the stuffy twilight of a back room opening off an Indian bazaar. He was wrestling with accounts which would not come straight. He toiled earnestly, piling up little heaps of copper and silver and counting them over and over again; but there was some queer muddle somewhere, and they refused to square with the roughly scrawled figures on the tally. He was baffled.

"Blockhead!" said his father tersely. "Blockhead!"

It was too much for the boy.

"Is it just, is it fair," he flamed out, "to call me 'blockhead' when you have never sent me to school? Let me go to Dohnavur and learn!"

If towards the end of a festival day a firecracker had walked across the street and gone off exactly under him, the father (man of repose as he was) would have jumped. He jumped now, mentally speaking, and he stared at the boy, flabbergasted. Dohnavur!

From that day on the idea laid firm hold of Kinglet, and when he saw his mother he told her of it. She saw in it the answer to the longings of her heart. (Of Star's, of course, she as yet knew nothing.)

But the letter, written by dictation, told Star that for some time—"for about three months," Star read with awe—her eldest boy had been beseeching to be allowed to go to Dohnavur. Might she bring him? Might she bring her second boy, too? She wanted to give them to God. Her husband had consented. When might she come?

"About three months." It could not be a mere coincidence; but Star, who has all her life gone to the bedrock of things, knew that such words as "I give my sons to God" might mean much or very little, and she did not, let it be remembered, know anything of all we know of those brave years. She did not know even that Mimosa was a worshiper of our God.

But she was sure that the Hindu father had no fear that his boys would become true and earnest followers of Christ. Had he not seen many a lad—his own nephews, for example—sent to school to be educated, who returned in the holidays to be subjected to all the ancient influences? How had they finally turned out? "Christians," perhaps, but keeping caste as of old—which, after all, is the great matter. They dealt with life in the Hindu way, not trammeled by Christian principles when they proved inconvenient. In fact, they were much like their forebears, only more or less educated. Who fears veneer? Not the Hindu father who knows the firm quality of the grain of the wood below. He would not deny that there have been a few exceptions, but they are not frequent enough to cause alarm.

Star wrote, therefore, explaining clearly that education *as an end in itself* was not a part of our thinking. And she told them our aim, even the conversion of the children: their deliverance from caste, and their devotion to the service of Christ. And she explained what the means were which we felt led most directly to this end.

It was a hard letter to write, for it seemed to shut the door and turn the key in the lock. It would have been harder still to write had Star known all that lay behind that letter of Mimosa's—seen the marks of the tears on it, felt the throb of the years in it. These, for the moment, were hidden from her. But she did greatly long to have the handling of her sister's boys. And there was one moving and heartening word in the original letter: Mimosa had referred to her childhood desire and said that perhaps it was to be fulfilled in these her sons!

Back went Star's answer, slowly as letters go through country places, and at last it reached Mimosa. Who with even the faintest flicker of imagination can fail to see her as she listened to the unimpressive reading of it by her husband? Star had thought it would almost certainly close the door. It had taken no common courage for her to write it. Now, all Mimosa's courage was needed to hear it read slowly and disapprovingly. Word by word it dropped into her heart like lead. It was impossible that her husband would ever agree to this.

But her Father *would* hear the prayer of His child. How often He had heard! Deep in her spirit there was peace; she prayed again.

And the impossible happened! We call the opening of the iron gate of Peter's prison a miracle. We know something of iron gates. We also know something of the Hindu, not as he is in the modern and modified India, but as he is in his own fastness of caste; we know that no iron gate that ever was hung is more firmly padlocked than is his mind where such things are concerned. Futile as the father had proved himself to be, poor-spirited as he flagrantly was, above all he was and is a Hindu! Had he said "No" he would have had his caste behind him. And yet he said "Yes"—and Mimosa wrote that they would come! Her heart sang with the birds that day.

Chapter Thirty-Three

As a Red-Hot Wire in the Ear

BUT he went back on his promise.

All this happened when I was away from home, held away by a particularly difficult work, so Star did not add these matters to my burdened days. Knowing I would be with her in whatever she did, she waited till she knew what was to come of it. For in our happy little world of Dohnavur we have never talked about being one—we *began* by being one. "Brown and white, white and brown, all mixed up together," as the children's song has it. But it is closer than that: we are "one'd."

For weeks she heard nothing. Then a piteous little letter came from Mimosa, dictated to her brother whom she had persuaded to do the writing. It told of the husband's consent, then refusal because of the caste's resistance; and yet, in the quietness of faith, she was apparently preparing for the hour when the gates would open. "Under hopeless circumstances he hopefully believed": it was like that. There was not a glimmer of light in her sky. But in order to be ready to start at a moment's notice she had sold her brass vessels, an Indian woman's most precious necessities. They had been her father's gift to her, part of her dowry, and she could never buy such again. Hereafter she must use cheap earthen pots. (She did not say this, but we knew it.)

With the money thus realized she had prevailed upon her worthless brother to escort them, "when her God should direct her goings." Part of the money was to be spent in providing for his little girls (whom he terribly neglected) and part on the journey. She hoped to come soon, she wrote.

Many days passed, and Mimosa did not come. What had happened? A thousand things might have happened; but of all vain ways of spending time, perhaps the vainest is to wonder over might be's, as one of the saddest is to dwell on might-have-been's.

Afterwards we heard it all.

The caste had continued its coercion. Held as she was, and unable to explain herself in the very least to them, she suffered. In this old land where days speak and the multitude of years teaches wisdom, the talk of the people is strewn with proverbs about the pain of cruel words: they are like red-hot wire thrust into the ear; like blisters of fire on the ear; like nails hammered sharply into the softness of unseasoned wood; piercing as arrows. Words hurt more than blows; to be hurt with words is like being beaten by wind and rain together. Every contact with the world outside her house now, as never before, made things bitter for Mimosa. And it had been bitter enough before. In speaking of it she said simply: "I lived before the Lord again with my sari in my hand."

Who could have succored her then but a Savior who had suffered? Are there not times in life when nothing less suffices? By the Gate that is called Beautiful we may find joyful access to the God of all beauty. But not until we reach the City whose every single gate is one pearl shall we find *only* joy as we enter in. Yea, and all who will live godly in Christ Jesus shall suffer persecution. Sooner or later we must all come to the place where we hear a voice—a voice that is deep with unfathomable pain—calling us to the fellowship of suffering.

But there we find Him. And who but Jesus—the crucified, risen Redeemer—could suffice us there?

"I have in my study pictures of Millet, Goethe, Tolstoy, Beethoven, and Jesus Christ in the garden of Gethsemane," wrote a Chinese student, not yet a Christian, to his friend in Paris. "After seeing a beautiful picture, reading some wonderful poetry, or hearing some exquisite music, my spirit goes out, not to Jesus, but to the pictures of the other famous men. But when my heart is in trouble, these can no longer charm: only my contemplation of Jesus in His agony in the garden seems able to bring me peace."

> "For hadst Thou passionless
>   Spent easy days, O Christ, known only joy's
>   dear kiss,
> Walked on safe sandaled feet
> In meadowlands—Ah, who that ever ran
> Naked across the plain,
> Scourged by the vehement, bitter rain,
> But turning to Thee desperate, would miss
> Something in Thee, yea, vital things? Tears
>   were Thy meat,
> A spear-stab Thy caress,
> Thou suffering Son of Man."

Chapter Thirty-Four

Bind on Thy Sandals

*A*T THAT time her husband was living in a town some ten miles distant from the caste village of her clan. She could have come to us without his knowledge; but, straightforward as her father, it never occurred to her to do so. Her loyalty to that feeble-spirited man, who mooned away his days and left her to keep the family, had never for one instant wavered. Of such fine stuff are the women of India made, trained through hard generations into a disciplined unselfishness that is surely matchless among the nations of the earth.

Then, suddenly, she knew she had to come. She could not explain this strong sense of being compelled, she only knew that it was so. "I *had* to come," she said.

And we who listened wondered if the angel who found Peter long ago had shone upon her and wakened her from an almost trance of prayer, though indeed it was no trance, for body and mind were strained to utmost activity. However it was, chains fell off from her. "Bind on thy sandals," said that calm angel long ago, so unhurried, though every moment was precious. Calmly she made her arrangements now; and, visibly escorted by the brother who had so often thrust at her (but invisibly, as we believe, by the blessed mighty angel) she passed through the various wards of her caste-bound little city. And the iron gate that led out of it opened, as iron gates do where angels are. Mimosa, with her baby in her arms and her three little sons walking beside her—while the brother she had bribed attended them—took the road that led to the town where her husband was, not knowing what would befall her there.

They were tired when they reached the town of the great Hindu temple. Go down those streets in the early morning and you will see haughty Brahman faces glancing at you superciliously from behind the iron bars that guard the verandahs where they sleep on polished wooden slabs. Rising on their elbows they survey passersby with a look that must be experienced to be understood. It is the very essence of distilled superiority. Walk down the amazing corridors of that amazing temple, and you will need to summon all your faith to believe that the day will ever come in India when justice shall run down as waters, and righteousness as a mighty stream.

To this town, in her weakness—a thing of shame as her people saw her—Mimosa went now, past the great temple walls; and she looked up at them. They had looked down on her boy when he rubbed ashes on his forehead. Let even the boldest look at them and they seem to turn his most tremendous assault to a shower of snowflakes. And as Mimosa walked past them, she felt her faith assailed from all sides by those enormous buildings. I have stood on the step leading into the inner shrine of that temple. I have talked with fierce and sensual men, and to some also of the kind who bring to remembrance the young man whom Jesus, looking upon, loved. But never once have I talked to one whose being was not visibly impressed by the influence of the massive piles about him. Mimosa felt its subtle forces now, and the presence of the man beside her accentuated this sense of impotence. He had tasted the good word of God and the powers of the age to come, and no change had passed over his spirit. In the long war between good and evil, who was triumphing? So far as she could see, the devil, not Christ.

Chapter Thirty-Five

Not in Despair

*S*HE reached her husband's house in the late evening, and immediately was flung body and soul into a very caldron of confusions. The place was boiling over with excitement, for the news of her intention had run before her and stirred up the sluggish husband and his neighbors, and the house filled in a moment.

"Stark madness—abominable, soul-defiling, caste-destroying! Better throw thy children in the river or a well, or toss them into the jungle." And they all raved together, heaping curses, protestations, denouncements on poor Mimosa's head, with great clamors of loud voices and a frenzied flinging about of arms and hands and glaring of angry eyes; and she stood undefended in the midst.

For hours the *furor* continued. They knew of the secret medicine the Dohnavur people used. It was a white powder. It was given to make people Christians. It would be given to the children just as, long ago, some such medicine had been given to the boys' unfortunate mother. Had she not been most peculiar ever since? The boys would clean forget everything good and destroy their caste by actions not to be tolerated. Kinglet listened to all this with open ears and a horrified soul. Was that what they did at Dohnavur? Then he for one did not want to go.

But Mimosa stood her ground. "Shall I throw my children, for whom I have worked as a coolie, to the river or the well or the desert? Nay, but I will go to Dohnavur and return."

At last, having shouted itself hoarse, the company dispersed, and, too agitated inwardly to touch food, though she held herself still before them all, Mimosa lay down beside her little boys and tried to sleep. She was oppressed, but not in despair. With the dawn she would rise and go.

But with the dawn, one who had never slept—Satan—arose and stirred the husband to fresh opposition. "I will never let thee go," he said. Then sturdy Mischief spoke his mind in decided tones. He said to his mother: "Tell Star I am only four and I have walked for ten miles, and my feet are sore. I will come another time." This gave the father his cue. Certainly the Fortunate Fourth would stay with him. As for their firstborn, nothing would persuade him to part with him, and he led him off and hid him away in a private room and turned the key in the lock, lest at the last moment he should change his mind again.

And now all was safe. This would bind the mother's feet, for what mother would leave her firstborn and her Fortunate Fourth?

And Mimosa, what could she do? The strange pressure, as if of a hand upon her pushing her forth, had not passed from her; she knew that she must go. But how, without her boys?

She stood silent, as is her habit in all moments of high tension. We who have seen her can see her as she stood speechless, gazing with dark, deep eyes into something not seen by men. What is it that we see when we are not here at all in the body but out of the body? The shouting about her sounded faint and far away. She was communing with her Father.

Were these children—whom He had given her and for whom strength to toil had been given year after year—were they to be taken from her one by one and brought up to follow that which she abhorred? Twice, for a few brief minutes, she had been given to drink from a cup of living water. Were her children to go thirsty all their lives? She knew there was more to drink than those few drops in the cup—there must be springs and fountains. Oh, the thirst of her years! Were her children never to drink and be satisfied?

But how could she leave two of them to the malice of those who would use the opportunity to the full? What might not be shown to them within one week in that wicked heathen town?

It is not the fashion to speak thus. We whitewash facts now, fearing to offend. But, deep under all, we know, and there are some who do not fear to say it: the blackest pages of our Bibles find illustration in every land where the fear of God is not. Sin may be covered with garlands of jasmine, but it is sin.

This was all open to the mother; but with a valorous faith, faith that could not be refused, Mimosa cast her treasures into the arms of God. She had the assurance that she must go on; but it rent her very heart, and she lifted up her voice and wept.

And as she went along the road, carrying her baby and leading her seven-year-old boy by the hand, she went on weeping, and her firstborn heard her voice and broke from his prison, for this was more than he could bear, and he raced after her. She heard his footsteps and stopped.

"Mother, mother, do not go," he cried most earnestly. "They will give the drugged medicine powder." For the talk he had heard had soaked into his soul.

She hardly remembers what she said, only she knows she did not try to persuade him to come. She was past talk now; she simply went on. And the boy went with her.

Then, raising her hands to heaven in a mute gesture of adoration, with one supreme act of faith she committed her jewel child, the little four-year-old from whom she had never been parted, to the special care of her Father and God, and set her face once more towards the journey to distant Dohnavur.

It was a weary walk for them all. They had left home after a scanty meal on the previous afternoon. The children had been given food on arrival at their father's house, but Mimosa had touched nothing either then or before starting. A bandy journey would follow, and then another trudge on the hot roads. It was a silent company that toiled, for they were too fatigued to talk; but they never thought of turning back.

Two evenings later, in the unannounced fashion of the East, they arrived at Dohnavur.

Chapter Thirty-Six

Mimosa?

I WAS in a far corner of the compound at the time; a scout flew to tell me. And, as I ran across the playground, detaining little hands caught at my sari and little dots of blue danced and tumbled around me, but I hardly saw them. I recalled a small, slim figure in its orange and crimson raiment and pretty silver bangles against the green shadows of the mango trees, saw the brave brown eyes trying to smile through tears, saw the little hands held up in a gesture of farewell. Fled were the twenty-two years like twenty-two minutes. Mimosa here!

"Where is she?" I asked the panting child who trotted alongside.

"On Premie Sittie's verandah."

A moment later I was there. Facing the door, as I went through it, stood a man—and in that flash of time two currents ran from him to me, joy and sorrow; but the sorrow flowed over the joy and ended it. "O Servant of Righteousness (his baptismal name), is it *thou*?"

Then the woman who was standing with her back to the door turned quickly—a tired, old, old woman. Mimosa? Where was Mimosa? The little girl of the bright raiment and the jewels and the tears, where was she? But in a moment she was in my arms like a long-lost child

found at last. Tears? There were tears, who could have re-
strained them? And through my own I saw her, an old,
tired woman, years and years older than I felt myself.

Beside her stood three boys, weary but polite, and in
her arms was a baby extremely impolite. He created a di-
version by wailing a vehement protest, and his mother
dashed the tears from her eyes with the gesture so well
remembered and comforted her baby, and peace reigned
again, and we all made friends.

Two of the boys were her little sons; one, from that
halfway halting place, was a nephew, notorious as a scamp-
ish young madcap, who had elected to come, "to see what
it was like," he said.

At first it was as if there was nothing left of that little
lost girl but the soft brown eyes. But gradually, as she rested,
there appeared slowly, as a face rising slowly through clear
water, the dear and familiar in this child of our desires.
The character was there, the quick intelligence, the wonderful look of spiritual apprehension that in childhood was
impressive in both sisters. But all was masked by age. Star,
two years older, looked much younger. Four times we had
been down with her to the borders of death; doctors had
given her up; only our hope held on. She can never be
strong, we are told, and she has often suffered; life has not
always been kind to her. But beside this wayworn woman,
Star looked as if she had glided down the smooth river of
the years in a cushioned barge. But the calm eyes of quiet
brown told of victory and peace: "As dying, and, behold,
we live."

Oh, what will it be when such as she bathe in the pool
of immortality? Will they rise with youth renewed, the

pain they wore so long stripped off like an encumbering wrap, the real essential spirit of the life lived here shining forth like a light through clear crystal?

What will it be, when they escape from the cramping ways of time and find themselves in the infinite? For the entrance of the greater world is wide and sure, and they who see the straitness and the painfulness from which they have been delivered must wonder exceedingly as they are received into those large rooms with joy and immortality.

Chapter Thirty-Seven

The End of a Golden Thread

WE had many talks together, and the talks came to be like looks through open windows into a house full of beautiful things.

I do not think that in the East such looks are often given. A shyness slips like a pane of glass between speaker and listener. Then a little breath breathes on the pane, and a fine mist clouds it. Then a curtain is drawn across, and no more is seen. So even a fugitive glance is something to be thankful for.

Thinking over these long looks that were really times of heart listening to heart, it seemed to me that something new had been given, even a very lovely story too good to keep to ourselves.

One evening, as we sat on a fallen block of stone, looking without speaking at the pink flush in the sky over the mountains, the question rose in my mind, How did Mimosa know what she ought to do and ought not to do in the little matters of life where compromise would have been so easy, and a narrow hardness so hindering and hurting to others?

The festivals, for example, that are part of Indian life as much as the pattern woven in the carpet is part of the carpet, so that you can hardly walk on the carpet without treading upon the pattern; and the little customs and courtesies that are like the dye in the colors—what of them? How can one walk at all without offence?

"When Kinglet was a baby, my sister-in-law asked me to come with her to the great festival at the temple by the sea, and all my neighbors and relatives went; yes, everyone went, and I went too.

"There was much brightness and a gaiety; but at night tom-toms and strange noises and a feel of something I did not like. I did not go ever again."

And the family ceremonies and feasts? "I always went if I could. But in the Ritual of the Corner while the women 'censed' the offerings, swaying the censer so" (and her arm swung gently to and fro), "then I waited outside. I waited while they marked Siva's sign upon their foreheads, and then I went in and joined with them in love."

And so it was all through. She could not tell me why she had felt some things impossible; it was just that she was not at home in that air, and the sounds were the voices of strangers.

The sun had set by now, the sky was like a great soft rose with a single star shining deep in its heart. I thought of Jenny Lind, of the story told in her biography of how one found her by the sea at sunset with her Bible open on her knee, and asked her how she came to abandon the stage at the very height of her fame.

"When every day it made me think less of this"—and Jenny Lind touched her Bible—"and nothing at all of that"—and she pointed to the quiet sky—"what else could I do?"

But Mimosa had no Bible. Would it have been strange

if she had missed her way?

    She had the end of the golden thread:

> "I give you the end of a golden thread,
>   Only wind it into a ball,
> It will lead you straight to Jerusalem's gate
>   Built in the city wall."

    Oh, need we ever fear? The least strand of that thread is enough to lead the one who holds it fast all the way home.

Chapter Thirty-Eight

"Farewell, Little Brothers"

ONLY a few days of rest, and the mother knew she must return. She could not rest with us while her little Mischief with his wide-open eyes might be seeing unforgettable things and hearing words no love of hers could wash from memory. Her baby had been taken, protesting indignantly, to our little hospital, and Vadivu had tended his hurts, for the hard life his mother was living had told very sorely on him. We wanted to keep him till he was well; but even those few days had changed him from a fretful, wailing, skinny scrap into something approaching a jolly baby boy. Even his mother's anxious eyes would light, till they shone like gentle stars, as she listened to the chuckles of this her unlucky, precious Fifth and saw him nod his bandaged little head when we asked him: "Tell us, little God's Gift, tell us, will you come back for the Christmas festival?"

We had dreaded the good-bye. The boys and their cousin (who so far has taken the law into his own hands and decidedly intends to stay) were with the others in the playroom when the time came for Mimosa to go. She had seen her own alone before; now she just looked in, all her hungry mother-passion in her eyes; but they did not see it. "Farewell, little brothers," she said, waving her hand to the whole company, indicating with a delicate, purposeful turn of the phrase that hers were ours and ours were hers, each and all included in that farewell: "Peace be with you, my little brothers."

And so she left us, loving and simple and very brave.

Chapter Thirty-Nine

"Send for Me: I Can Come"

BUT she is back again.

For on a good day a letter came from her, saying: "I beseech you to send for me. My coming is possible." How? What had happened? Hardly daring to believe the thing could be, we sent our faithful Pearl, fellow-worker for nearly thirty years.

And she returned with Mimosa and the sturdy four-year-old and the ten-months-old baby boy, and with a wistful and dear little maiden, the elder brother's neglected little daughter whom Mimosa had befriended. "I could not leave her. I could not have left a little puppy dog to be lonely and half starved," she said. But Mimosa looked almost frightened in her wonder and her joy. She looked as if she felt anything might happen any minute to end it. It has taken a whole month to wash that look from her face.

One day her husband came here. He had not gone near her upon her return, so she had felt at last, with a sudden courage, that he did not care for the disgrace of owning a wife whose leanings were now known to the world. And that was why she had felt free to rise up and come.

She told him now that she would return if he wished it, but not just yet. She must learn—yes, she was learning to read! She could no longer go on without being able to read the Bible. All those years she had felt her way like one blind, groping and stumbling; now that her eyes had been opened, she must see clearly, she must know. "When I am established I will return."

It was the last thing he desired, but he went away, and now her hope is that he will come back and wish to learn himself. For he could not help being impressed by the astonishing happiness of everything he saw. It was the evening hour when he came into the Boys' Compound. Kinglet was playing football with the other biggish boys. Music and another were careening about on an old tricycle, and Mischief was dashing giddily around as driver of a team of horses with jingling reins. Later on he had them to himself for a talk. "Do you not wish to come back with me?" But the boys were silent; they did not want to hurt him, but they did not want to go. Then Music had a happy thought. Why this dilemma? "Be God's man and come with us," he said.

Music has beautiful earnest eyes, like the eyes his mother had when she stood by the mango tree and tried not to cry. With these eyes looking into his, his father could answer nothing. Perhaps they will draw him to come.

But he left us that day without food; he would not stain his caste by touching our food, and some are praying for another miracle.

Not till yesterday did I hear the end of Mimosa's journey home. The story dropped by accident among some other tellings.

She had left us without money. Not a word had she said, and we did not know. Afterwards a fear shot through us lest it might be so, and we sent a servant after her with enough to take her home. But he loitered by the way, and it did not reach her.

The first part of her journey was easy, for she traveled with one of our family; but after the bullock cart and train were left behind there was a fifteen-mile walk, and, carrying her baby boy and her little bundle of things, Mimosa became suddenly faint.

"Father, I am tired. Kindly give me strength to walk."

She sat down by the road, a desolate figure, alone as no Indian woman cares to be alone on the road, for her brother (who had been paid to escort her to us) had gone home a week before.

"Father," she said, looking up in the old way, "Father, I am tired. I spent all I had in taking the boys to Dohnavur; I cannot hire a cart. But indeed it is necessary that I should reach my home. Kindly give me strength to walk."

For a little while she sat there, saying softly, "Father, Father," and the word comforted her, and she got up and walked, though slowly with pauses to rest, the remaining ten miles.

But she was exhausted when she reached home. She lay down on her mat, with her Fifth beside her, and she longed for a drink of water.

Presently, to her relief, a relative, hearing she had returned, came in, and, touched by the sight of her fatigue, drew water, lighted a fire, and put things in proper order for the evening meal.

Mimosa lay and watched her from her mat. It was getting dark, and we know how depressing twilight and tiredness together can be. Soon the house was dark save for the light of the poor little fire made of a few small bits of brushwood, gathered before she left home and left in readiness. There was no gleam of polished brass vessels, no brightness anywhere. She missed her little Music. The unfortunate Fifth was tired and cross—poor little lad, it was not his nature to be cross, but he had had a good deal to put up with—and she, his mother, was tireder than he; but deep in her heart she was utterly content.

"If only I could be sure of seeing them even once in the year," she had said to Star in a moment of almost weakness of resolve; but she had rallied at once. She knew it would not be easy to come even only once a year; but they would be happy and learning to be good. What did anything else matter?

Now she lay and thought of them, pictured their every action, following them through their day with loving, loving eyes, and then, with that act of committal which had brought peace to her so often before, she looked up through the dull air of the dull little house. "To You, Father." The word has a gesture of its own; it is the gesture of a little child who has learned to give up something it would have liked to keep.

The Fortunate Fourth was retrieved. That very decided young man had made up his mind to rejoin his mother, which settled matters so far as he was concerned.

Then, as the days wore on and her husband took no notice whatever of her, she said she had begun to wonder whether he truly had, for the present, at any rate, tired of the disgrace of such a peculiar wife. And at last, like the glorious silver shining of the dawn star in these skies of great stars, a thought rose slowly as in some far, dim horizon of the mind, and it rose and rose and swam upwards till it became familiar, beautiful, a star of hope indeed. She would go back to Dohnavur! She would learn to read, that the Book of God might open to her! She would receive the spiritual washing! After that, God would show her what to do. Yes, she would rise and go. "And so I have come," she said as she ended her story.

Chapter Forty

Love Will Find a Way

$\mathcal{B}$UT it was only the ending of one chapter and the beginning of another, and this, the last that may be written now, centers round a certain glorious Sunday evening when, with the western sky aflame, we streamed forth to the side of the Red Lake under the mountains (the lake shown in *Lotus Buds,* in the picture called "God's Fire").

There, as we stood in a long, curved line on the long, curved bank, scores of little children scattered among grown-up people and boys and girls, Mimosa—while her husband stood looking on in bemused quiescence—walked solemnly into the water to receive her baptism.

To some who had lately joined us it was just that ever-joyful thing, a Christian baptism, but to us who saw her standing, as it were, at the end of a long avenue of years, to the invisible angels and to their Lord and hers, how much more—oh, how much more it was than pen can write or tongue tell!

And now she is back in her bigoted Hindu world, and she writes that some wonder, some scoff, and some are listening a little. Her husband, whom she has set her heart on winning, feels her a disgrace, but the amazing thing is that he still owns as his wife one who has so shamed his caste (which is *not* one of the more tolerant which allow a woman to remain within the fold even after baptism). Her life cannot be easy. But then, she has not asked for ease; she has asked for the shield of patience so that she may overcome.

So we do not fear at all to leave Mimosa's story here, with the first happy ending, that promises another happier, most happy forever. And this first chapter of a book that is still being written goes forth with a great joy and with two earnest intentions—to comfort, if it may be, some who, depressed by the perplexities of these days, are almost tempted to think our Lord is not in His world now as He was in olden time; and to win help for those who need it.

Will the first be in any wise fulfilled? Can one consider this solitary Indian woman—protected, comforted, sustained, fed with bread the world knew not of, given to drink of fountains in the desert—without feeling that the love of God has many ways of working, and may be working now unseen through all the clamor and the sadness of a foolish generation? Is not such a story a witness to the Invisible?

Are there those for whom we have long prayed for, who seem beyond our reach now? *Love will find a way.* Are we discouraged because we do not see our expected signs, and the solid rocks seem to be sinking under shifting sands? It is not so. Love is mighty and must prevail. Terrible in judgments, marvelous in lovingkindness, Love will find a way.

Out in these corners of the earth, those who are face to face with the old elemental forces of sin know what it is to shiver at times with a sense of the almost omnipotence of the god of this world. Is there not comfort for us in this story? In and out of the deep, dark places of heathendom— yes, and as truly among the garish lights of a Christendom that has lost its first warm love—*wherever* there is the least, the faintest response to Love, there Love will follow and find, for nothing in heaven or earth or under the earth is impossible to Love.

And will not my second intention find fulfillment somewhere? Will not prayer that can be as a shield in battle, as dew in heat, as a cool wind on a breathless day, as the light of moon and stars at night, be round about any anywhere who, enchanted by a glimpse of the loveliness of Christ, are following Him today—dear, unknown fellow-lovers? For God has other Mimosas.

Afterword

ONE day, about a year ago, two of us went to Mimosa's village, and I stayed with her. I saw then, for the first time, the room mentioned in Chapter 9. It is narrow and low and airless, and when the small, heavy door is shut, it is quite dark. It is the only place where Mimosa can be alone.

Is her story true? Although the foreword said it was, some have wondered if it could be so. When first I went into that room I stood astonished. In the dark corners I could see the dim shapes of huddled-up sacks and a pot or two. It was unbelievably stuffy. I could hardly breathe. Myheart almost questioned then the things that I had heard. Can it be here, O Lord of life and light and liberty, that Thou didst meet her so often? Can such dinginess be indeed the place of Thy Presence?

She was out busy cooking in the verandah that ran around the little courtyard at the time. She thought I would like the door shut. "And when thou hast shut thy door" has always been one of her words, so she softly shut the door. Then not a breath of air came in and not a ray of light. In that hot darkness I stood, and thought of the angels ascending and descending not on some ladder set up under the stars, but here, in this strip of room . . . "Take off thy shoes from off thy feet, for the place whereon thou standest is holy ground."

And a new insight, like the sudden flash that sometimes lights the evening sky in these tropical lands and
shows kingdoms beyond the clouds, was granted in that
moment. I knew, not by faith now, but as it were by sight,
that our Lord Jesus Christ can do anything, keep anyone,
shine anywhere, succor in spite of all the forces of the en-
emy, comfort in any circumstances. Verily, circumstances
are nothing to Him. He is King of them all. The material
is powerless to cramp or to subdue. It is naught. The Spiritual conquers every time.

Many ask about her husband and children. Her husband is still what he was, and she still hopes; her boys are
with us. A little daughter has been given to her. Lately,
because of her courageous witness, her house roof was
burned down. She wrote on a postcard, covered with
crowded Tamil, a vivid account of the fire, ending thus:
"But through bitterness comes sweetness."

Amy Carmichael
Dohnavur, 1930

*A*S this book, written over thirty years ago, goes out once
more it seems necessary to add to the author's own after-
word and bring the story up to date, incorporating in this
note details of what she herself wrote, above, when the
sixth reprint was made.

Mimosa had the joy of seeing her husband turn to the
Lord, and later receive baptism. She continued to live in
her village with him but frequently visited us in Dohnavur.
On one occasion she arrived just at the time when Golden,
a leprosy patient, was longing to see her. A Tamil version of

Mimosa's life had been read to Golden, and she was eager to see with her own eyes the one who had held fast to her faith in Christ for over twenty years, without human help. Her face shone when Mimosa was brought to her bedside, realizing that it was God Himself who had made this meeting possible.

The translation of the book into various languages, however, though it brought blessing to many, was followed by sharp spiritual attack upon Mimosa herself, an attack which lasted for over a year before she came through to peace and victory.

In 1938 she became seriously ill and was brought to our Hospital, where she rested in peace until the trumpets sounded for her and she went in to see the King.

Four of her sons are with us now, trusted and loved fellow-workers. Her daughter, who is married, is living elsewhere and so is her youngest son, born after the book was written. Her husband is spending his old age here in Dohnavur. The eldest of their grandchildren (Kinglet's son) has begun to take his share in the work among the boys.

Star was called Home in May 1939, only six months after her sister. The story of her early years has been written in the book *Ploughed Under*. God called her to serve Him in Dohnavur, chiefly among the young boys, but her love reached out to all, so that her life is a radiant memory to those who knew her. Though sheltered from the physical hardship and care that were Mimosa's lot, Star in her warfare for souls knew the wounds and piercing sorrows that such work brings.

For both sisters as they entered into Life the words of *Pilgrim's Progress* were true: "You must there receive the comfort of all your toil, and have joy for all your sorrow; you must reap what you have sown, even the fruit of all your prayers and tears and sufferings for the King by the way."

Barbara C. Osman
Dohnavur, 1958

The Dohnavur Fellowship

The work in Dohnavur, South India, began in 1901 when Amy Carmichael, while doing itinerant evangelistic work, came to know that little girls were sometimes taken and trained as dancing girls for the Hindu temples—which meant a life of evil for them. Wherever she could, she saved children from this fate, and, with her as "Mother," the Family in Dohnavur began. This was the thrust of the Dohnavur ministry in 1924 when this account of the life of Mimosa was written. But naturally many changes have since occurred.

The work in Dohnavur continues, but now the Fellowship members are all of Indian nationality. They do not belong officially to any of the organized churches, but in fellowship with others of God's children, they seek to make His love and salvation known to all whom they can reach.

The dedication of girls to the temples is now illegal, but the Fellowship provides a home for children who might otherwise fall into the hands of people who would exploit them in some way.

Girls of all ages from babies to teenagers form a large part of the family in Dohnavur. The need to care for them continues until they are securely launched elsewhere or else have become fellow workers. The aim is still to bring them up to know and love our Lord Jesus and to follow His example as those who desire not to be served but to serve others.

The hospital treats patients from the surrounding countryside. They are from varied religious backgrounds—Hindu, Muslim, Christian. They include rich and poor, highly educated and illiterate. Through this medical work God continues to bring to us the people we long to reach, those whose need is for spiritual as well as physical healing.

Boys are no longer admitted, but the buildings they occupied are now put to full use. In 1981 the Fellowship in partnership with other Christians formed the Santhosha Educational Society to administer a co-educational English-medium boarding school, primarily for the benefit of the children of missionaries of Indian nationality. The buildings provide facilities for over 600 children now studying there. Their parents come from Indian missions and organizations working in many parts of India, including tribal areas.

In matters of finance, we follow the pattern shown from the beginning of the work. Amy Carmichael rejoiced in her Heavenly Father's faithfulness in supplying each need. We praise Him that His faithfulness is the same today.

The Dohnavur Fellowship
Tirunelveli District
Tamil Nadu 627 102
India

Books by Amy Carmichael

PUBLICATIONS

Fort Washington, PA 19034

This book is published by CLC Publications, an outreach of CLC Ministries International. The purpose of CLC is to make evangelical Christian literature available to all nations so that people may come to faith and maturity in the Lord Jesus Christ. We hope this book has been life changing and has enriched your walk with God through the work of the Holy Spirit. If you would like to know more about CLC, we invite you to visit our website:

www.clcusa.org

To know more about the remarkable story of the founding of CLC International we encourage you to read

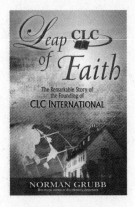

LEAP OF FAITH

Norman Grubb

Paperback
Size 5^1/$_4$ x 8, Pages 248
ISBN: 978-0-87508-650-7
ISBN (*e-book*): 978-1-61958-055-8

AMY CARMICHAEL OF DOHNAVUR

Amy Carmichael

Amy Carmichael, born in 1867 in the village of Millisle, Ireland, gave herself unconditionally to Christ. She went first to Japan and following a short term in Ceylon, presently Sri Lanka, she landed in India in 1895 and remained there without a single furlough until she died in January 1951.

Paperback
Size 5¼ x 8, Pages 432
ISBN: 978-0-87508-084-0
ISBN (*e-book*): 978-1-61958-072-5

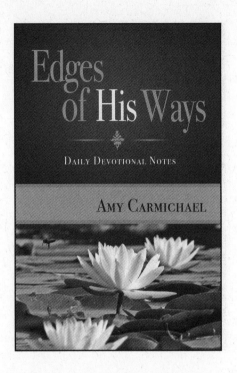

EDGES OF HIS WAYS

Amy Carmichael

Even when struggling with illness, Amy Carmichael frequently sent reflections and revelations from Scripture to missionaries and orphans within Dohnavur Fellowship to encourage them. Her collection of devotional thoughts will share with you pieces of who God is so you can better trust the completeness of His purposes for your life.

Paperback
Size 5^1/$_4$ x 8, Pages 237
ISBN: 978-0-87508-062-8
ISBN (*e-book*): 978-1-936143-61-0

HIS THOUGHTS SAID . . . HIS FATHER SAID

Amy Carmichael

Amy Carmichael voices the inner thoughts we all have that bring discouragement, doubt and fear, and gives a godly response that dispels these false ideas. Read a short portion in a free moment or pore over its pages prayerfully for hours as it provides bite-sized, biblical answers to your unspoken questions.

Mass Market
Size 4¹/₄ x 7, Pages 110
ISBN: 978-0-87508-971-3
ISBN (*e-book*): 978-1-61958-035-0

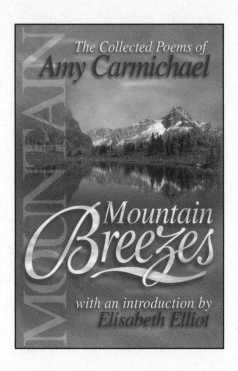

MOUNTAIN BREEZES

Amy Carmichael

Amy Carmichael was an instrument chosen by the Lord in her teenage years to minister unto the people of India. Her books have comforted and challenged many, and reveal a life and work fully dedicated to the glory of God. *Mountain Breezes* is a collection of poems that will inspire and bless readers.

Paperback
Size 5¹/₄ x 8, Pages 472
ISBN: 978-0-87508-789-4
ISBN (*e-book*): 978-1-61958-098-5

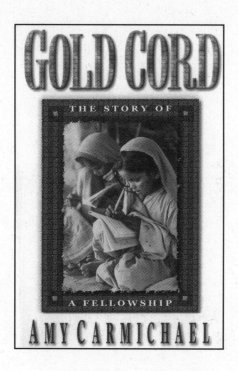

GOLD CORD

Amy Carmichael

The Dohnavur Fellowship is a group of Indian and European men and women working together in South India. Its friends wanted to know how it began, and asked for something that would link up the stories already written: "What [kind of cord] holds you together?" Dohnavur answered, "A gold cord."

Paperback
Size 5¹/₄ x 8, Pages 413
ISBN: 978-0-87508-068-0
ISBN (*e-book*): 978-1-61958-071-8

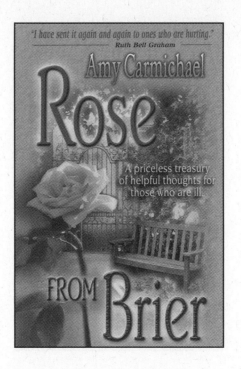

ROSE FROM BRIER

Amy Carmichael

Amy Carmichael wrote *Rose from Brier* after reflecting that most books of comfort for sick people are written by the well and so miss their mark. Since pain is not always physical, this is a book for all who suffer, as it has been written *by* the ill, *for* the ill.

Mass Market
Size 4^1/$_4$ x 7, Pages 208
ISBN: 978-0-87508-077-2
ISBN (*e-book*): 978-1-936143-74-0

IF

Amy Carmichael

Amy Carmichael questions whether we allow our doubts and disappointments to hinder our faith, or do we really know Calvary's love? In a series of statements and common situations, a Christ-love of forgiveness and strength is meant to mend our hearts and encourage others, because of what He has already done.

Mass Market
Size 4¹/₄ x 7, Pages 70
ISBN: 978-0-87508-071-0
ISBN (*e-book*): 978-1-936143-51-1